THE COMPLETE GUIDE TO
PUPPY CARE

MARK EVANS
ANIMAL CARE

THE COMPLETE GUIDE TO
PUPPY CARE

MITCHELL BEAZLEY

To my pack: Sarah, Finlay, Jessie and Gorbachov

Executive Art Editor: Vivienne Brar
Commissioning Editor: Samantha Ward-Dutton
Project Editor: Jane Royston
Designers: Paul Griffin, Nina Pickup
Production: Juliette Butler

First published in Great Britain in 1996 by Mitchell Beazley,
an imprint of Reed Consumer Books Limited,
Michelin House, 81 Fulham Road, London SW3 6RB and
Auckland, Melbourne, Singapore and Toronto

ISBN 1-85732-799-3

A CIP catalogue of this book is available at the British Library.

Printed in China

Contents

Introduction

Dogs are such a familiar part of our society that – all too often – we take their presence in our homes and our lives for granted. However, despite the way that we may treat many of them, pet dogs are not furry little people. They have unique physical and mental needs, and are not born 'pre-programmed' to understand human ways.

It is a tribute to their extraordinary tolerance and adaptability that so many dogs are such a pleasure to own, and cause little or no trouble to their owners. Yet there are plenty of human–dog relationships that are far from perfect, in which neither the dogs nor their owners get as much from sharing each others' lives as they should do.

Just as young puppies should become used to all kinds of people and other animals from an early age in order to grow into sociable and well-adjusted adult dogs, so we should try to look at life from their point of view. When interacting with a dog, it is important to interpret his body language to understand how he is feeling and what he is trying to say. Sadly, breakdowns in communications do occur, and animal-rescue centres are full of dogs who have lost their way in life. In many cases, their only crime was to have been too dog-like and not human enough!

Choosing a puppy

The best relationships between people and dogs are built on solid foundations, laid well in advance. Thorough research and planning when deciding on a breed or type of dog will help you to select a puppy who is likely to grow and develop into an adult dog well-suited to you and to your lifestyle.

Many people choose their canine companions on the way they look, but this kind of approach is really no more sensible than agreeing to marry someone having only seen a photograph of a close relative!

For instance, West Highland white terriers are very beautiful dogs and a popular choice as family pets, but – even though small – they can be quite a handful to live with and look after. Despite their appearance, these dogs are in temperament much more like other typical terriers than teddy bears, and some experts consider many individuals to be far from ideal pets for families with young children. By contrast, some cross-breds and mongrels of my acquaintance – who have what you might call 'unusual' looks – are some of the most well-adjusted family dogs I know.

Well before you obtain your puppy, his probable temperament, the amount and type of exercise that he will need, his coat-care requirements, feeding costs and many other practicalities must all be taken into consideration. They may seem obvious, but such factors are often disregarded in the pursuit of a particular type of dog.

Practical preparations

Once you have decided on the puppy that you would like, preparing yourself and your home for his arrival will take time. You will need to make your house and garden safe and secure, you must select and buy all the necessary care products, and you will have to decide on what and how to feed your puppy.

With these aspects well-organized, you can then devote yourself completely to helping your puppy settle into his new surroundings when he first comes to live with you.

Caring for a puppy

There is no one perfect way to look after a puppy. All dogs have a great deal in common, but the individual whom you adopt will be unique, with his own personality, particular likes and dislikes, and unique behavioural quirks. As a result, his precise care needs are likely to differ from those of any other dog. Being sensitive to his requirements and adapting the way that you look after him to meet them is an art that you will learn only through practical experience.

Although you may turn to this book – or to any number of dog experts – as necessary for advice and guidance, you are the only one who can make the final decisions relating to your puppy's care. Like the rest of us, you are bound to make mistakes but, by using this book as a guide, keeping an open mind, adopting a flexible approach to the care of your puppy, accepting the limitations of your own skills, knowledge and abilities, and being prepared to ask for help when necessary, you will be able to identify and remedy any mistakes quickly. More importantly, you will be much less likely to make them in the first place.

Responsible dog-ownership

The information and advice given in this book does not constitute a complete set of rules dictating how to look after a puppy. It is simply a guide to the most important issues that – in my view – all dog-owners

The author walking near his home with his three-year-old labrador retriever, Jessie.

need to consider very carefully both before and after a canine companion comes into their lives.

As your puppy's owner, you must be prepared to make decisions on his behalf, just as you would do for a child. You will be responsible for much of the time for what he does and where he goes to do it, and you will need to teach him to be well-mannered and calm when he is out and about, as well as keeping him mentally stimulated and fulfilling his physical needs.

You will also be responsible for your puppy's health. Some accidents and illnesses are obviously unavoidable, but implementing good preventive healthcare throughout your puppy's life is vital. This will involve carrying out regular health-checks and monitoring his inputs and outputs: namely, what he eats, drinks and the waste that he produces. Sudden alterations in any of these – as well as unexpected changes in his behaviour – may be early signs of

illness. Detecting these early will enable you to take action on your puppy's behalf to prevent him from suffering unnecessarily.

No matter how good you think you may be at caring for a dog, try not to be complacent. No-one is a perfect dog-owner, and no-one ever will be. The fact is that, the more we learn about dogs, the more we realize how much more there is still to find out. All of us should therefore be humble enough to adapt our views on dog care as our experience grows and when new scientific knowledge becomes available.

Using this book

The following pages contain a mixture of the most up-to-date information that I have been able to find, along with personal views based on my experience of living with and treating dogs of all kinds.

The book follows a logical progression through the conception, birth and very early days of a puppy, to the preparations that you will need to make for your own puppy's arrival (to avoid any confusion, I have referred to your puppy as 'he' throughout). Next comes detailed information on practicalities such as toileting, basic training and exercise, and a final section covers all aspects of preventive healthcare to keep your puppy happy and healthy. Ideally, you should aim to read the book all the way through first, and then refer back to specific sections as a general guide.

While good preparation is the key to successful dog-ownership, nothing I have said here and none of the decisions that you make about your puppy's care are set in stone. Your puppy will not have read this book, and he may not react to new situations and new experiences in exactly the ways that I have suggested. Be flexible, and be ready to change the way that you do things if necessary.

There is no way of being faultless dog-owners, as our dogs cannot tell us what they think of the way that we look after them. We therefore have to rely on a mixture of scientific knowledge, experience and basic common sense to do the best we can.

This book provides a general philosophy on puppy care, but only you can decide exactly how you are going to look after your own puppy and what kind of lifestyle you will be able to give him. Above all, you must remember that his needs are mental as well as physical. This means altering his day-to-day routine, continually providing him with new experiences and ensuring that his life is full of fun.

Remember that variety will be the spice of your puppy's life – as well as of yours.

What is a dog?

Pet dogs are remarkable mammals, whose origins can be traced back thousands of years to the time when ancient peoples first developed relationships with wolves. Today, they are cherished by millions of families. However, despite the way we tend to nurture them throughout their lives, dogs do not remain babies for long.

The evolution of the pet dog

Dogs have been our faithful companions, servants and protectors for thousands of years, and yet it is only relatively recently that we have known for certain the wild animal to which all pet dogs are related. Take away their names, and ignore what they may look like, and all the breeds and types of pet dog you have ever seen are actually one and the same species. And what a remarkable species it is: perhaps no other on earth comes in so many different colours, shapes and sizes.

THE WOLF

If it were not for the wolf, there would be no Afghan hounds, labradors or Yorkshire terriers. And there would be no need for this book!

The relationship between man and wolf goes back at least 500,000 years, but for most of that time the wolf remained a wild animal, hunted for its pelt. The moment at which it was first tamed, or domesticated, is hard to pinpoint, but the earliest indications that we have are the bones of a wolf buried alongside those of a person, presumably its 'owner', from a grave 12,000 years old. This animal may actually not have been a wolf at all, but an early pet dog, although its anatomy was virtually identical to that of the local species of wolf, so it is hard to be sure.

It is difficult to imagine the magic moment when a person first touched a living wolf, and decided to feed and protect it rather than to kill it. Perhaps such friendly encounters between man and wolf occurred in several places at around the same time: we may never know. But experts believe that the pet dog was 'created' in Asia and the Near East, where the wolf is a much smaller animal than the American variety that is most familiar to us today.

OTHER ANCESTORS?

Modern genetics has established that the primary – and possibly the sole – ancestor of the dog is the wolf. However, some experts believed that other species known to be able to interbreed with the wolf could also have a claim to the ancestry of the pet dog.

Wolves are pack animals, and sleep, hunt, eat and rear their young together. They are able to communicate through body language, scent messages and vocalization, and all the pack members abide by a strict code of discipline enforced by the most senior wolves.

The coyote and jackal

The red wolf was once thought to be a separate species and therefore a potential ancestor, but is actually the result of breeding between the wolf and the coyote.

Konrad Lorenz, who won the Nobel Prize for his work on animal behaviour, thought that many dog breeds were derived from crosses between the wolf and the jackal. He based this on the behaviour of certain breeds, such as the German shepherd, which he considered jackal-like: outgoing, but tending to become over-attached to people. However, modern research has ruled out the jackal as an ancestor.

The pariah dog, singing dog and dingo

Some of the most ancient types of pet dog still exist today in the wild. These include the pariah dog of India, the tiny New Guinea singing dog and the dingo of Australia. However, none of these can be considered true ancestors of today's pet dogs; they are primitive breeds that have reverted to their wild state.

DOMESTICATION

The wolf, as it was 12,000 years ago, must have almost domesticated itself, because – as far as we are aware – man had simply never tamed a wild animal before.

Whatever the details of the domestication process, the wolf was already well-adapted to take its place in human society. A wolf pack is ruled by the alpha-male and alpha-female, and the other pack members defer to them. Today, a dog's human owner takes on the role of pack leader, and the dog is naturally 'programmed' to form a strong relationship with that owner.

Just like their wild ancestors, pet dogs are pack animals by nature and will develop close ties to those with whom they live. An individual dog will look to his human family for leadership and protection, and will offer unconditional companionship, devotion and loyalty in return.

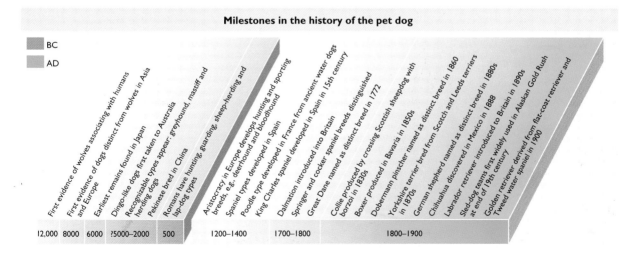

Milestones in the history of the pet dog

BC

AD

First evidence of wolves associating with humans	First evidence of dogs distinct from wolves in Asia and Europe	Earliest remains found in Japan	Dingo-like dogs first taken to Australia	Recognizable types appear: greyhound, mastiff and herding dogs / Pekinese bred in China	Romans have hunting, guarding, sheep-herding and lap-dog types	Aristocracy in Europe develops hunting and sporting breeds, e.g., deerhound and bloodhound / Spaniel types developed in Spain	Poodle type developed in Spain / King Charles spaniel developed in France from ancient water dogs / Springer and cocker spaniel developed in Spain in 15th century / Dalmation introduced into Britain / Great Dane named as distinct breed in 1772	Collie produced by crossing Scottish sheepdog with borzoi in 1830s / Boxer produced in Bavaria in 1850s / Dobermann pinscher named as distinct breed in 1860 / Yorkshire terrier bred from Scotch and Leeds terriers in 1870s / German shepherd named as distinct breed in 1880s / Chihuahua discovered in Mexico in 1888 / Labrador retriever introduced to Britain in 1890s / Sled-dog teams first widely used in Alaskan Gold Rush at end of 19th century / Golden retriever derived from flat-coat retriever and Tweed water spaniel in 1900	
12,000	8000	6000	?5000–2000	500	1200–1400	1700–1800	1800–1900			

Changes in anatomy

A wolf, the dog's primary ancestor, is instantly recognizable: the long, pointed muzzle, pricked-up ears, thick coat and bushy tail all contribute to its familiar outline and appearance. However, the wolf was not always that shape and size. Every part of its body design – including the shape of its teeth, the size of its heart, the precise anatomy of its eyeballs and the colour and length of its coat – has been constantly restyled over the last 50 million years through natural selection, the way in which animals evolve to become perfectly adapted to their natural environment.

But what about the pet dog? As soon as the wolf was first tamed, man started to interfere with the process of natural selection by choosing which animals bred together, and by providing their offspring with life support in the form of shelter, warmth, protection and food. The wolf began to change in both shape and temperament. The first change to its anatomy, which still persists today, was a reduction in the size of the jaw and, in particular, the teeth. Even large dog breeds such as the Great Dane have much smaller teeth than the wolf. The remoulding process did not stop at the head, and, over the past 12,000 years, the first dogs have been transformed into hundreds of breeds.

Changes in behaviour

Through manipulating the breeding of his dogs, man has gradually managed to adapt the highly developed, all-round hunting skills of the wolf to produce types of dog with particular hunting abilities.

The various hound types specialize in finding prey: some, like the greyhound, rely on their good eyesight and fast running; others, such as the bloodhound, use their refined sense of smell. In the retriever, the wolf's habit of bringing his food back from the kill has been exaggerated; while in the setter and pointer, the wolf's tendency to hold back from the kill until all the pack members are in position has been retained. Almost all the components of co-operative hunting behaviour (except the kill) are still visible in the sheep-herding

In appearance, this male golden retriever has much in common with his ancestor the wolf. However, his teeth are smaller, his ear flaps so large that they hang down, and his coat is one colour. Other dogs may look very different, but the basic design of their bodies is the same.

muzzle

eye

upper jaw

ear flap

lower jaw

abdominal wall

flank

rump

withers

neck

tail

hip joint

shoulder joint

upper forearm

thigh

knee joint (stifle)

chest wall (rib cage)

elbow joint

point of hock (heel)

forearm

wrist

hind foot (with four clawed toes)

forefoot (with four main clawed toes)

dogs, such as the border collie. Particularly obvious are the stalk and the 'eye', or fixed stare, used as a psychological weapon by wolf and sheepdog alike. Only in the livestock-guarding breeds, such as the maremma and the Pyrenean mountain dog, has the entire hunting instinct been suppressed: these dogs appear to regard all animals as their friends!

The modern breeds

The separation of dogs into breeds is a fairly new idea, dating back little more than 150 years. Indeed, many of our most popular breeds – the golden retriever is one example – are relatively modern creations.

Whether morally right or wrong, the development by man of the pet dog in all its modern forms is one of the most bizarre events in the history of the natural world. Who would believe that a wild wolf, a tiny chihuahua and a huge Great Dane are all products of the same original 'blueprint'? The body parts of the different breeds may be all kinds of shapes and sizes, but the overall layout is basically the same.

ANCIENT BREEDS

Many of the body types that we recognize in our modern breeds were already present 3000 years ago. The earliest divisions were into hunting, herding and guarding types. The most ancient breed is probably the greyhound, closely followed by the saluki, both of which originated in the Middle East. The heavy mastiff type probably originated in Asia, and was recorded as arriving in Egypt, brought by the Hyksos people, in approximately 1600 BC. Some people may claim many other breeds to be ancient, but they are in fact modern 'reconstructions' of much older types of dog.

A great proliferation of breeds took place in the late Middle Ages (13th–15th centuries), led by the aristocracy who produced different kinds of dog for hunting and other sports. New blood was also brought into Europe by knights returning from the Crusades. For example, the spaniel type was probably derived from crosses between the thickset European pack hound and the elegant Middle Eastern greyhound.

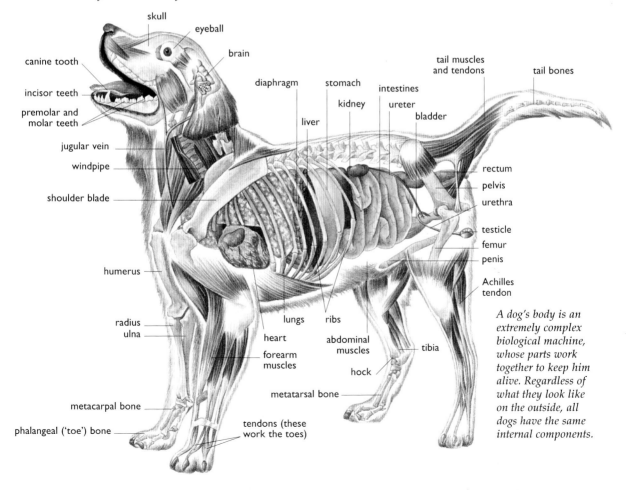

A dog's body is an extremely complex biological machine, whose parts work together to keep him alive. Regardless of what they look like on the outside, all dogs have the same internal components.

Your puppy's life starts here

If you have ever had a baby, or you know someone who has, this is a subject that I am sure you will have talked about many times. The mere concept of one living animal developing and growing inside another fills most of us with wonder. Whether you are the husband, a friend or a relative of the mum-to-be, you just have to become involved!

The early days of a puppy's life, both before birth and after it, are no less exciting – perhaps even more so, as everything happens so much more quickly with dogs than it does with people.

Where does it all begin?

Very sensibly, the majority of dog owners do not breed their own puppies, and so miss out on experiencing the early development of their dogs. If you plan to invite a puppy into your life in the near future, or he is already with you but you wish you had been there when his life began, this part of my book is for you.

Over the next few pages, you will discover some of the fascinating events that take place, from the fertilization of the puppy's egg, through pregnancy, birth and the first eight weeks of life. With us, it all starts with a kiss. With dogs, it's not so different.

The mating behaviour of dogs is all their own. Having ejaculated his sperm and 'tied' with the bitch, the dog may step over her back so that he ends up facing away from her.

A bitch and dog during the 'tie'

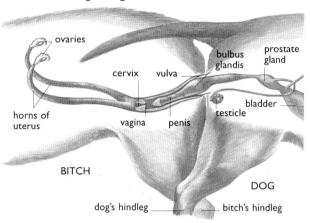

The 'tie' between the bitch and dog occurs as a part of the dog's penis – the bulbus glandis – swells inside the bitch's vagina. The muscles of her vulva constrict to hold it in place.

THE MATING GAME

Adult male dogs are generally sexually active and interested in mating at any time, whereas adult female dogs (bitches) will only mate at certain times of the year. Called 'heats', these sexually active periods last for just a few days and normally occur about once every six months (see pages 122–3).

Most matings are planned by responsible owners, and generally take place at the male dogs' homes. Unfortunately, some matings are far less formal events arranged by the dogs themselves, often staged in the most public of settings.

The sexual act

If the timing is right when a dog and bitch meet, they will first greet each other nose-to-nose, and will go on to sniff each other's groins more intensely than during a normal greeting. If all goes well, they will begin to play. The bitch will keep turning her bottom towards the dog, and will hold her tail over to one side.

After a period of this initial foreplay, the dog will stand alongside the bitch, facing the same direction as her with his tail held erect. He should wait for her to move her tail to one side again before mounting her. Intercourse itself is a fairly hectic thrusting affair that lasts just a few minutes. The dog will ejaculate his sperm within the first 80 seconds.

The dog then dismounts, but his now swollen penis normally remains locked in the bitch's vagina for up to an hour in what is known as the 'tie'. He ends up in the opposite direction to the bitch and hopes that she still likes him, because some bitches can become active while tied and may try to bite their mates.

During the tie, the male ejaculates quite a large volume of fluid to help wash his sperm into the bitch's uterus. Conception is possible, however, even if the dog and bitch do not tie.

Ovulation

The bitch's eggs are produced in her two ovaries. At ovulation, which occurs approximately three days after the beginning of a heat, an unknown number of eggs will start to be released to begin their journey down the tubes that connect the ovaries and the uterus.

While this is happening, and for the next few days, the bitch will happily mate many more times (even several times a day) with the same or any other dog to whom she takes a fancy – bitches and dogs have been shown to have personal preferences when it comes to choosing their mates!

If the mating has been organized by the bitch's owners, she will probably be offered the chance to mate just twice with the same dog. Those bitches who arrange their own matings may have intercourse with a number of different dogs of all shapes and sizes.

LIFE BEFORE BIRTH

Puppies are largely helpless at birth, and have to rely almost entirely on their mothers for the first three to four weeks of their lives. This is because they spend a comparatively short time – just nine weeks on average – in their mothers' wombs. In those weeks, however, an intriguing series of events begins to unfold.

Conception

Once an egg has been fertilized by a sperm, a reaction occurs that prevents any other sperm from entering the same egg. In theory, a bitch who produces a litter having mated with a number of dogs could have had each of her eggs fertilized by a different father.

Some bitches will give birth to just one or to only a few puppies, while it is possible for other bitches of the same breed to have litters of up to 14 puppies.

The journey to the uterus

For the first two weeks after conception, each puppy-to-be, or embryo, is barely larger than a pin-head. First of all, the embryo travels down the tube that connects the ovary to the uterus. On its journey, the single cell from which the puppy will eventually be formed divides first into two, then into four, then into eight cells and so on, until it turns into a solid but still microscopic ball of cells.

When all of the embryos – each one destined to become a puppy in the same litter – reach the uterus, they spread out evenly along its two sides and then embed themselves in its wall.

The developing embryo

As each embryo develops further, some of its cells begin to create the body of the unborn puppy. Other cells start to form the sac membranes that surround it, as well as the placenta that will connect its blood system to that of its mother.

At this stage the embryo is barely recognizable as an animal, let alone a puppy, but by about 20 days after conception it will have the beginnings of a head, and its backbone will have started to develop. The placenta is not yet functional, and the embryo obtains most of its nourishment from a built-in food source called the yolk sac.

By the time the placenta starts working, the embryo is the size of a hazelnut. It floats in a sac of fluid, and is connected to its placenta by a rope of blood vessels called the umbilical cord. The limbs, head and eyes then begin to develop rapidly, and by the end of about four weeks all the puppy's organs have been formed, although they are not yet fully developed.

At this stage each embryo is just 2.5–3 cm (1–1¼ in) long, curled up in the so-called foetal position.

HOW MANY SPERM ARE NEEDED FOR FERTILIZATION?

Only one sperm should actually be required to fertilize one egg, but scientists estimate that perhaps one million sperm are needed to create a suitable environment for this to occur. An unknown number of eggs may be fertilized, but there is no guarantee that all of them will develop into puppies.

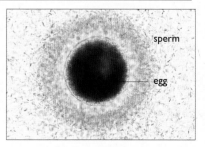
sperm
egg

HOW FAST DOES A FOETUS GROW?

The following facts relate to a medium-sized dog.

• Week three: the embryo is 5 mm (⅕ in) long and the two sacs that surround it have formed.

• Week four: the embryo is 2 cm (⅘ in) long and the first signs of developing limbs can be seen.

• Week five: the foetus is 3.5 cm (1⅖ in) long and the eyelids and ear flaps are visible.

• Week six: the foetus is 6 cm (2⅖ in) long and the individual toes and genitals are well-developed.

• Week seven: the foetus is 10 cm (4 in) long. Hair is starting to develop at this stage, as are the puppy's future markings.

• Week eight: the foetus is 15 cm (6 in) long and has hair and paw pads.

The foetal stage

From four weeks after conception to birth at about nine weeks, the puppy is referred to as a foetus. During this period the foetus's organs mature and it grows rapidly, doubling in length once between day 28 and day 40, and again by day 49. Male and female foetuses can be distinguished at about day 30; live puppies can be born from day 54 onwards.

Touch • This is the first sense to develop, and is present from about 28 days onwards. What use a foetus makes of the ability to feel its surroundings is not known, but it may control limb movement, which can be felt from the seventh week.

Taste • This sense probably also starts to function before birth, enabling the foetuses to taste the amniotic fluid in which they are floating. They may be able to learn a little about the foods that their mother is eating, as certain flavours can survive digestion and reach the amniotic fluid.

Balance • This begins to function eight weeks after conception.

Sight and hearing • These two senses develop at a later stage; a newly born puppy is both deaf and blind.

THE PREGNANT BITCH

The first external sign that a bitch has conceived usually comes after four to five weeks. Her nipples enlarge and become bright pink, and the hair around them recedes slightly. She may also produce a slight discharge from her vulva. Initially her weight gain will be small, so she will move around as easily as before.

Most foetal growth occurs in the last three weeks of pregnancy, and this is when the bitch will really start to put on weight (see opposite, below), with her abdomen swelling noticeably if she has a large litter. Some bitches produce a watery fluid from their nipples at around day 40 of pregnancy, and milk from day 55. Others may only produce milk just before the birth.

Confirming pregnancy

Breast development, abdominal enlargement and weight increase can all occur in bitches going through pseudo-pregnancy (see page 123), so these signs are not guarantees that a bitch is carrying a litter. A vet can use the following techniques to confirm pregnancy.

Abdominal palpation • It is possible in some bitches to feel the foetuses. This is easiest at about 28 days into pregnancy (later on, it becomes more difficult to distinguish the individual foetuses).

Ultrasound examination • Although it is possible to detect pregnancy just 16 days after ovulation,

Ultrasound examination of a bitch uses an advanced piece of equipment similar to that used on a pregnant woman. The procedure is quite painless, and most bitches readily accept it.

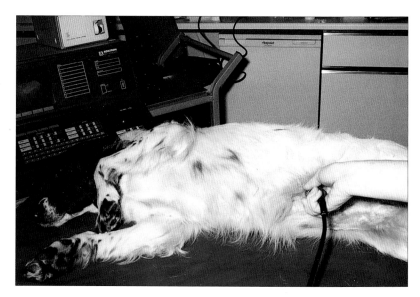

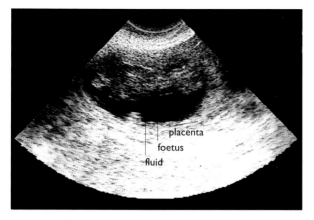

The image created by an ultrasound machine can be very difficult for inexperienced eyes to interpret. This picture shows a developing foetus on day 28 of pregnancy.

A cut-away view of the bitch's uterus

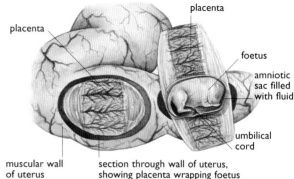

The bitch's uterus is Y-shaped, and the developing foetuses are spread along both arms of the 'Y'. Each foetus is totally enclosed within its own life-support system inside the uterus.

an ultrasound examination is normally carried out at or after day 28 of pregnancy.

Blood testing • This is possible from day 30.

Taking an X-ray picture • After day 45 of pregnancy, an X-ray picture of a pregnant bitch's abdomen will reveal the tiny foetal skeletons.

Listening for foetal heartbeats • This can be done using a stethoscope during late pregnancy; the foetal heart-rate is faster than that of the mother.

ECG (ElectroCardiogram) • It is possible to measure the electrical activity in the hearts of the foetuses using special equipment.

The last week of pregnancy

In the days before the birth, a bitch will generally search for places in which to have her puppies. She may tear up her bedding to make a 'nest' and may be very restless, whining or crying repeatedly. She may also show aggression towards other dogs and possibly even people. She is currently the victim of competing instincts: her attachment to her human owners and their home is fighting against her natural inclination to leave her 'pack' and dig herself a secure whelping burrow elsewhere, as feral dogs usually do.

Most of a pregnant bitch's weight gain occurs after week five (left). Her food intake should then increase so that, at labour, she is eating up to 60 per cent more than when mated.

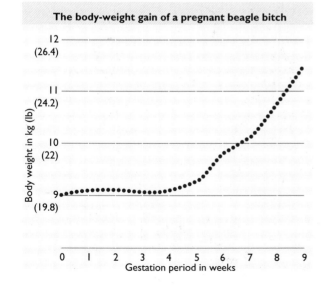

The body-weight gain of a pregnant beagle bitch

Body weight in kg (lb)

12 (26.4)
11 (24.2)
10 (22)
9 (19.8)

Gestation period in weeks
0 1 2 3 4 5 6 7 8 9

HOW LONG IS PREGNANCY?

From the time that the ovaries are stimulated to ovulate eggs, the length of pregnancy in bitches is remarkably consistent at 64, 65 or 66 days. However, because sperm can remain alive and capable of fertilizing eggs for about a week inside the bitch's uterus, the apparent length of pregnancy will depend on when the mating occurred in relation to the time of ovulation.

For example, an early mating before ovulation has occurred may result in an apparently long pregnancy of up to 72 days, while a seemingly very short pregnancy of just 56 days may be the result of a late mating after ovulation has taken place.

Birth

Completely enclosed in their individual life-support systems, the unborn puppies, or foetuses, enjoy a fairly stress-free existence. In the darkness of their mother's uterus, they are kept warm, nourished and protected. But nine weeks – give or take a few days – after their parents mate, these helpless foetuses take part in initiating a remarkable chain of events that results in their physical and forceful eviction from the security of their mother's body. Labour, or whelping, has begun. The puppies are about to be born.

Pre-birth behaviour

Thanks to ante-natal classes, most people have a good idea of what to expect during the birth of a baby; yet perhaps knowing too much is one of the reasons why so many human mothers-to-be are apprehensive about labour. For bitches who are pregnant for the first time there are of course no such classes, so we have to assume that, although they must feel peculiar and have a stomach ache, they have no idea what is going to happen next. They just get on with it and leave their owners to do the worrying!

A first-time canine mother experiences all kinds of new sensations prior to labour. Her pulse quickens, she may pant erratically and her body temperature will drop by a degree or so. With her sex hormones

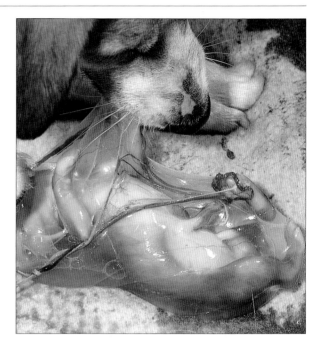

Enclosed inside his amniotic sac, this newly born puppy is unable to breathe. His mother quickly releases him, using her teeth and tongue to remove the membranes.

A cut-away view of the bitch's birth canal

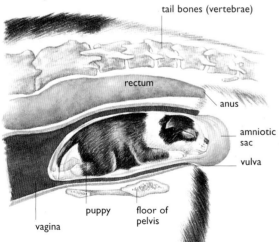

tail bones (vertebrae)

rectum

anus

amniotic sac

vulva

puppy   floor of pelvis

vagina

The presence of a puppy in the part of the birth canal within the pelvis causes the bitch to strain. The puppy's delivery is eased by the slippery membranes that still surround him.

disrupted and so many other major physical changes affecting her body, she can be forgiven for behaving slightly strangely. Every bitch is different and there are no rules, but most bitches tend to go off their food, become restless and attempt to dig up or shred their bedding – perhaps more through pain than due to a biological instinct to make a nest. Some bitches become more aggressive than normal in the presence of any strangers, but may cling to their owners.

GETTING READY

In the last hours of pregnancy, the bitch's body rapidly prepares itself for action.

Having been closed during pregnancy to seal off the uterus, the bitch's muscular cervix now undergoes complex changes that will allow it to open fully when the time is right for the first puppy to be born. Her uterus starts to contract, and, having supplied each foetus with life-giving blood during pregnancy, the individual placentas begin to 'unplug' themselves from the uterine wall.

The birth canal

For the puppies to be born, the bitch's birth canal must now adapt to allow their safe passage. Her pelvis and its ligaments begin to relax, and her vagina, vulva and the other tissues surrounding them soften so that they can stretch as each puppy is forced through.

Preparing to be born

The creation of a suitable birth canal is only part of the story. The foetuses themselves must also get ready to become puppies capable of surviving outside their mother's body. Two of their most serious problems will be breathing and coping with the cold. Of course, living underwater inside their mother's uterus, there is no way of testing their lungs before birth. However, alterations in the levels of certain hormones in their bodies are thought to help in causing the necessary changes in their lungs that will allow them to start working first time on demand. And, to prepare for a colder environment than the one to which they are used, the foetuses rapidly create energy stores that can be burned off after birth to produce body heat.

In order to avoid becoming jammed halfway out, each foetus must also adopt a streamlined pose ready to 'dive' forwards or backwards through the birth canal if necessary. During pregnancy, the foetuses usually lie curled up, facing the mother's spine. In the last hours before birth, they uncurl their bodies, straighten their legs and roll over.

THE FIRST PUPPY

The strong contractions of the uterus finally push the first foetus through the cervix and into the mother's pelvis, and, as soon as she feels it there, the bitch begins to strain. There is now no turning back. By contracting her abdominal muscles at the right time, she pushes the foetus on through her birth canal.

Rupture of the 'water bag'

The first thing to appear at the bitch's vulva is likely to be a 'water bag': one of two fluid-filled sacs that have surrounded each foetus during pregnancy. This

A newly born puppy behaves like a heat-seeking missile and will instinctively stay close to his mother's body. Here he will find food, as well as the warmth that is vital to maintain his body temperature at this early stage.

sac may break within the birth canal but, if not, it will either rupture as a result of the pressure of straining, or will be broken subsequently by the bitch licking and chewing at it. We must assume that, to her, the bag is a strange and irritating object sticking out of her bottom that needs to be removed. She can presumably have no idea of what is actually inside it.

The delivery

With each contraction and each strain, the puppy moves on, his passage through the birth canal made easier by the lubricating effect of the sac membranes that still surround him. Most puppies are born head-first, but as many as four out of 10 puppies enter the world backwards during normal deliveries.

The bitch has to push hard in order to squeeze the puppy's head through her birth canal, but the rest of the body usually follows fairly quickly. From the onset of straining, it generally takes a bitch between 20 minutes and one hour to deliver her first puppy.

Gasping for air

Fortunately, most bitches are naturally gifted 'do-it-yourself' midwives, and the newly born puppy will be quickly licked into life.

The bitch's first priority is to get him breathing as quickly as possible. To prevent him from suffocating, she nibbles away at any remaining sac membranes and rasps them from the puppy's face using her rough tongue. And she doesn't stop there: by continuing to lick her puppy in order to clean him, she stimulates him to breathe.

The puppy's first breath is usually taken within 60 seconds of his birth, and is more of a gasp than a breath as he inflates his lungs for the very first time.

Drying off

The bitch's next urgent task is to dry off her puppy thoroughly: left wet, he will rapidly chill and may die. So she continues to lick the puppy and moves him towards her breasts, where he will find both warmth and food. The bitch also breaks the puppy's umbilical cord – if it has not already been broken – by chewing through it with her back teeth.

GOOD FOOD

Before birth, each puppy has his own placenta and is enclosed within two fluid-filled sacs. After the birth of a puppy, parts of the placenta and the sacs remain inside the bitch. Called afterbirths, they are pushed out by the bitch either within a few minutes of the puppy or later on during the whelping, when the afterbirths from several puppies may be delivered at once.

All the afterbirths should be delivered within two hours of the last puppy being born. At whatever stage they appear, the bitch's first reaction may be to eat them. Resembling pieces of shrivelled liver, they may look absolutely revolting to us, but they are actually very nutritious. In the wild, the cubs' afterbirths are an important source of food for a wolf bitch in the days after giving birth when she is unable to hunt.

BROTHERS AND SISTERS

While mum may take a short rest to clean herself up, puppy number one searches for a nipple and begins taking the most important meal of his life – colostrum.

This first milk contains substances called antibodies which, if consumed within 24 hours of his birth, will provide the puppy with short-term immunity against the diseases to which his mother is immune, such as infections against which she has been vaccinated (see pages 120–1).

However, the bitch may not have much of a rest. The second puppy – if there is one – could be born within five minutes, but normally arrives about 30 minutes later, and will receive the same meticulous attention as the first puppy. That may be it, or there may be more. Any further puppies could all follow in quick succession, or they may be delivered more erratically. There is no set pattern, but in most cases it is all over within 12 hours.

After whelping, a bitch has many new responsibilities. She must protect, feed and clean up after her puppies, and will do so even though she may be exhausted. She relies on her natural instincts to do the right thing by her new family: inevitably, some bitches make better mothers than others do.

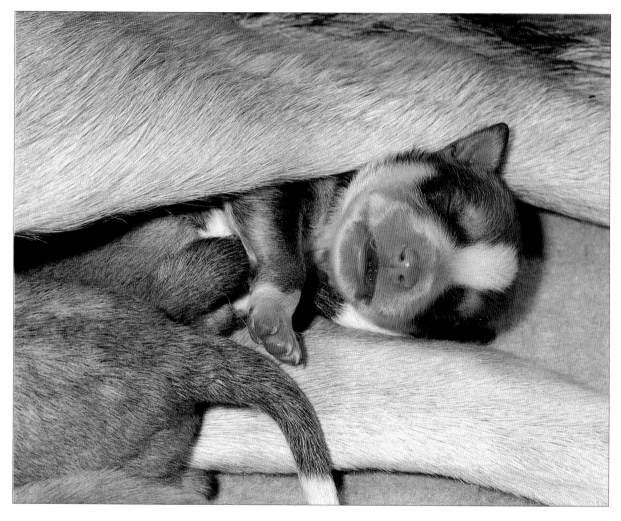

THE NEW FAMILY

Very tired and hungry after a long whelping, the bitch has not only herself but also a new family to care for. The puppies may have left her body, but they are still entirely dependent on her for warmth, food and protection. They are blind, they cannot hear properly and they have little or no co-ordination. Unable to do more than wriggle at first, they spend most of their time feeding or sleeping huddled together in a heap.

Homing instincts

Each puppy has a built-in reflex that helps to keep him close to his mother and his litter mates. Known as the rooting reflex, this is a complex but life-saving response that makes a puppy turn towards and push into any warm object near his head. That warm object

These puppies are just a few hours old. Warm, well-fed and comfortably sheltered between their mother's hindlegs, they can sleep peacefully until it is time for their next meal.

is obviously most likely to be either his mother's body or one of his brothers or sisters. As a result, the writhing litter of puppies tends to stay together and close to the warmest part of the mother: her breasts.

But what happens if a puppy becomes separated from the warmth of his family? Well, he uses one of his other great assets: his voice. A very tiny puppy can make a surprising amount of noise, and there is no way that the mother of a lonely, distressed and cold puppy can ignore him for very long. She knows that peace and quiet will only be restored when he is returned to the scrum.

Early life

Many people believe that dogs are born either 'good' or 'bad'. As you are about to find out, however, nothing could be further from the truth.

Over the following pages, you will discover that all puppies go through several major phases of development. By familiarizing yourself with these, you will begin to appreciate what to look for when choosing the right person to breed your puppy (see pages 48–9). You will also learn that you have a crucial role to play in helping your puppy to develop into a confident adult dog and a happy and well-adjusted member of your family.

PHASES OF DEVELOPMENT

The development of a puppy is usually divided into four fairly distinct phases, as follows.

Neonatal phase • In the first and second weeks after birth a puppy is virtually helpless, and is only capable of taking in very limited information about the world around him.

Transition phase • This phase coincides with the third week of life, when a puppy's eyes and ears begin to work and his behaviour is affected by all manner of external influences.

Socialization phase • This generally occurs between four and 12 weeks of age, when a puppy learns how to become a social animal: first with his litter mates, and then with people and other animals.

Juvenile phase • This developmental period starts at about 13 weeks and extends until a puppy reaches sexual maturity. The end of this phase will vary considerably from breed to breed. It may be as early as six months for a chihuahua, one year for most medium-sized breeds and up to 18 months for giant breeds such as the Irish wolfhound. The length of the juvenile phase may be somewhat arbitrary for individuals who are neutered before they reach puberty. It also depends on the sex of the puppy: in females, the phase comes to an abrupt end with the onset of their first season, or heat, whereas male puppies normally start to show an interest in sexual behaviour from about four months of age onwards (see pages 122–3).

A good start in life

Some people maintain that the behaviour and temperament of an adult dog are largely determined by his breed, but such a view implies that genetics is the only important factor that determines the behavioural development of dogs. Breed differences are indeed significant when deciding what kind of puppy you should choose, but it is also true that even two dogs of the same sex and breed may be very different in character. Genetics does play a minor role in the temperament differences between dogs of the same type, but of

Very young puppies, such as these one-day-old Welsh corgis, do little more than eat and sleep. Warmth is vital, and a litter will often huddle in a 'sleep heap' like this one to conserve body heat.

From week four onwards, socialization with other dogs – as well as with humans – is an important part of development, and will affect the puppies' behaviour as adults.

Early experiences

The first four months of a puppy's life are especially important; his experiences at this stage will have a profound effect on the way that he will behave both as an older puppy and as an adult dog.

As puppies should ideally go to their future homes when they are between seven and eight weeks old (see page 68), the responsibility for ensuring that a particular puppy is exposed to the sort of experiences that will help him to develop properly must be shared by his breeder and, of course, by the puppy's new owner. If you decide to take on a young puppy straight from the breeder, that will be you. Although you will only start to care for your new puppy when he is seven to eight weeks old, you can still have an important influence on his earlier development by carefully choosing a breeder who will give him the right care and attention, and a suitable environment in which to live.

CHOOSING THE RIGHT PUPPY

If you plan to take on a young puppy, you should select a breed or type of dog that is well-suited to your circumstances and to your lifestyle (see pages 42–7). Many people are drawn to a particular breed on looks alone, but your dog's temperament will be far more important to you in the long term. All young puppies are appealing, but you must also consider what sort of adult a dog of the breed that you like will become.

much greater significance is the specific cocktail of experiences that individual puppies encounter during their puppyhood and adolescent years.

Many – perhaps most – behavioural problems in dogs stem from inappropriate or restricted treatment during their early lives. Most of these problems can be cured with the assistance of a professionally trained animal-behaviour expert, but it is obviously much easier and a great deal less stressful for all concerned if they are prevented from occurring in the first place.

RESEARCH INTO BREED BEHAVIOUR

Our understanding of the phases of puppy development owes a great deal to a piece of scientific research called the Bar Harbor project. Over a period of 17 years, the effects of early experience and genetics on the behaviour of five breeds – the beagle, the American cocker spaniel, the fox terrier, the Shetland sheepdog and the basenji – were investigated. Many of the dogs studied were cross-breeds, resulting from planned matings between the breeds. They were selected because all the dogs needed to be about the same size, but with markedly different temperaments.

There has to date been much less research into the development of toy breeds, giant breeds, or even of the medium/large breeds such as the golden retriever, the labrador retriever and the German shepherd, all of which are popular family pets.

There is no doubt that the precise timings of a puppy's developmental phases – particularly the juvenile phase and the major milestones that occur within it – do vary from one breed to another. The timings given on the following pages should therefore be taken as rough guides only.

Week one

A newly born puppy is barely recognizable as a dog. His head is round and appears far too big for his body, his chest is barrel-shaped and his legs are short and stumpy. Almost completely helpless, he is entirely dependent on his mother. He cannot even control his own body temperature, which at first is lower than that of a normal adult dog. As a result, the new puppy needs constant contact with his mother and/or litter mates in order to avoid becoming seriously chilled.

Sleep and food

The first 36 hours of a puppy's life are critical, as his heart, lungs and liver all have to make major changes in the way they function to cope with life outside the protected environment of his mother's body.

For most of this time, a puppy will simply alternate between two activities: sleeping and feeding. After a burst of repeated bouts of suckling on the first day, feeding will occupy around 10 to 20 per cent of his time for the first week. For 80 to 90 per cent of the time, he will be asleep. Even when sleeping, a puppy is growing and developing. His body constantly twitches, jerks and stretches, as if he is dreaming.

During their first week, puppies spend 21 of every 24 hours sleeping. Meanwhile, the bitch's uterus begins to return to normal: this process will take three months to complete.

THE BRAIN OF A NEWBORN PUPPY

A new puppy has a very immature brain: it is hard to detect any electrical activity at all inside his head! However, the part of the brain that controls his sense of balance, heartbeat and breathing is working. So too is the major nerve that transmits the sense of touch from the nose, although pain is probably only felt as a general sensation. The puppy's face is an expressionless 'mask', and his eyelids and his ears are closed. At this stage, the world is a kind of sensory desert to him.

This activity helps to develop his nerves and muscles, and will continue until about the fourth week, when sleep starts to become more peaceful.

Simple reflexes

Almost all the puppy's early behaviour is founded on basic reflexes. As soon as he is born and released from the sac membranes by his mother, he will demonstrate the rooting reflex, a side-to-side motion of the head that stops when he contacts one of his mother's teats (see page 19). The powerful sucking reflex then takes over. The puppy will also knead his mother's breasts with his front paws to help to stimulate the flow of milk.

If the puppy accidentally falls on his back at the end of a bout of feeding when his stomach is full, another reflex movement ensures that he is soon the right way up again. Picked up by his neck – something that his mother will do to retrieve him if he becomes separated from his litter mates – he will curl up into a ball so that he is easier for the bitch to carry. By the end of the week, this reflex will have changed, and the puppy will straighten out his hindlegs when grasped by the neck.

By this stage he will be able to move around a little on his own by 'rowing' with his forelegs. If repeatedly stimulated by his mother's tongue, he may travel as far as 3 m (10 ft) by this method.

Sensory development

Touch • A puppy's sense of touch is fairly well-developed even at birth. At a few days old, he can distinguish textures, and is able

It is wonderful to witness the very natural way in which a bitch suckles her new puppies. By kneading her nipples, the puppies help to release the flow of milk.

to tell the difference in feel between a piece of soft bedding and rough matting.

Smell • The puppy's sense of smell helps him to find and then 'home in' on his mother: within just a few days, he will have learned her personal odour and will move towards her whenever he smells it. Some experts believe that puppies may even find their mothers' odours comforting. To test this theory, a biologist called Michael Fox perfumed a bitch's abdomen with aniseed. He discovered that after a few days the smell of aniseed alone had a calming influence on her pups, whereas no such effect was found if the mother had not been treated in this way. Presumably, therefore, the puppies had learned the association between the smell of aniseed and the availability of milk.

Voice • Even though they may not be able to hear themselves, very young puppies can make a wide variety of sounds (their precise vocal abilities will depend on their breed). Whines, screams, grunts and mews are all part of their repertoire, and will provoke an instant response from their mother. The sudden reaction of most adult dogs to these sounds suggests that they are almost 'pre-programmed' to recognize the noises of a helpless puppy in distress. Perhaps the fact that their ears are in tune with the high-pitched sounds is one reason why it is so easy to attract a dog's attention using a squeaky toy.

The mother's role

The most important figure in a newborn puppy's life is his mother. She will spend virtually every minute of the next few days with her litter. For the first 36 hours or so her mammary glands will contain colostrum (see page 18), which differs in composition to the milk that she will produce for her puppies later on.

The bitch may be extremely defensive of her litter, particularly in the presence of other dogs, and at this stage most mothers naturally want enough seclusion to allow them to get on and look after their puppies. The bitch not only feeds and protects them, but also looks after their personal hygiene. Through grooming her puppies by licking them with her tongue, she stimulates them to go to the toilet. She then eats whatever the puppies produce in order to keep the nest clean and hygienic.

Vital statistics

Weight at birth

Toy breeds: 100–400 g (4–14 oz).
Medium-sized breeds: 200–300 g (7–11 oz).
Large breeds: 400–500 g (14 oz–1 lb).
Giant breeds: over 700 g (1½ lb).
The skin and hair of a newborn puppy account for almost one-quarter of his total body weight. Most puppies double their birth weight in the first 10 to 12 days.

Heart-rate • Less than 130 beats per minute initially, this increases to over 200 beats per minute by the age of two weeks. It decreases to the adult level of 100–130 beats per minute by the age of 12 weeks.

Breathing rate • Approximately 12 breaths per minute at first, this increases to 15–35 breaths per minute by the age of two weeks.

Body temperature • This is about 35.8°C (97°F) at birth, and then increases (after one to two weeks) to about 37.7°C (100°F) by the age of four weeks. It subsequently rises to the normal adult level of about 38.6°C (101.5°F) by the age of six weeks.

A one-week-old Welsh corgi puppy is 9 cm (3½ in) long.

Week two

In this part of the neonatal phase (see page 20) the puppy develops rapidly, with most of the important changes happening under his skin. By the middle of week two he should have doubled his weight at birth.

The puppy is still totally dependent on his mother. He is still incapable of either urinating or defecating voluntarily, and his mother will continue to groom away and swallow all his body waste.

Learning to crawl

To move around, the puppy will have progressed from the undirected 'rowing' method used during the first week of his life (see page 22) to simple crawling. If he is picked up, he may make stepping motions with his forelegs even at this early age. By the end of this second week, his hindlegs may also be able to step when his body weight is supported. This shows that

When the bitch returns to her puppies from a short period away, she will check them over and then encourage them to move just enough to allow her to settle down next to them.

BRAIN DEVELOPMENT

The electrical activity in the puppy's brain is still barely detectable in the second week, because few of the connections between nerve cells (which allow nerve impulses to pass) have been made. Sleep is still full of twitches and jerks, and the part of the puppy's brain that stimulates wakefulness remains poorly developed. As a result, he will still sleep for much of the time.

the nerve connections and reflexes that will ultimately allow the puppy to walk, trot and run are already forming in his spinal column. At this stage, however, he is incapable of walking because the muscles in his legs are not strong enough to support his weight.

Keeping warm

When the bitch leaves the nest, as she will now do voluntarily from time to time, her puppies crawl into a huddle or 'sleep heap'. This is not for social reasons, because the puppies are scarcely aware of one another at this stage. Instead, as they are still unable to control their own body temperatures, huddling together is a very good way of conserving heat.

A greedy puppy trying to feed for that extra bit longer may remain dangling from one of his mother's nipples as she moves away from the nest, and may be dragged out of it as a result. His body will start to chill very rapidly, and the puppy will begin to cry and twist from side to side, as if making rooting head movements (see page 19). His mother will quickly realize that he is in distress, and she will return to pick up the wayward puppy carefully in her mouth and lift him back into the nest.

However, a puppy who is warm and has been recently fed will now tolerate short separations from his mother and litter mates. At this age puppies seem to have very little sense of place, and depend upon just a few simple features of their environment – such as warmth and their mother's smell – to provide comfort and reassurance.

They may appear to be great friends, but these puppies are barely aware of each other's presence and sleep together simply to stay warm. However, their eyelids are about to open, enabling them to see each other for the first time.

Eye-opening

Towards the end of the second week, the world of simple certainties comes to an end as the puppy's eyes begin to open (in some breeds – such as the terriers – eye-opening is often delayed until the third week).

At first, the eyes are cloudy and greyish-blue in colour, and it is doubtful whether a puppy can see very much straight away.

A two-week-old Welsh corgi puppy is 11 cm (4½ in) long.

Week three

So many changes take place in the puppy's third week that it has been separated out as a distinct stage of development, called the transition phase (see page 20). Brain function is now further advanced, and the puppy is beginning to discover all kinds of connections between various parts of his surroundings.

New abilities

These are generally simple links, similar to the one made between the smell of his mother's body and the availability of food that already existed back in week one. However fundamental they may be, these new abilities enable the puppy to make greater sense of his environment. He is now better able to control his own body temperature, and is capable of moving around more deliberately. It is also possible for him to crawl backwards as well as forwards. Other, more precise, voluntary movements begin to occur as nerve connections are made between the puppy's limbs and his brain.

Sensory development

Sight • The puppy's eyelids are now fully open, but his eyes are probably not yet capable of producing a clear and focused image. Although he will show awareness of bright lights, a puppy will not blink at sudden movements at this stage.

Hearing • Closed since birth, the ear canals now open, allowing the puppy to hear what is going on around him. Loud noises will produce an obvious

Now that he is able to see and hear to a limited degree, a three-week-old puppy's world is full of surprises – including his brothers and sisters!

'startle' response: a puppy repeatedly exposed to such a stimulus at this age may develop a tendency to nervousness later on.

Voice • Many puppies will start to bark for the first time during the third week. Presumably, with their ears functioning, they can now hear this noise as well as the other sounds that they make.

Smell • The puppy's sense of smell has been present from the time of birth (see page 23), but is now well-developed and more advanced than either his hearing or his sight. As a result, the three-week-old puppy will spend a considerable amount of his time sniffing his surroundings.

HANDLING A YOUNG PUPPY

Even as early as the third week, a puppy can benefit from a little handling. Although simple cuddling is beneficial, it is also worthwhile placing the puppy on his back and gently holding him there for a moment, or holding him in mid-air.

Although he may become slightly upset, this type of mild stress has been shown to have a positive effect on a puppy's character. It can improve both his problem-solving ability and his emotional balance later in life, particularly if he tends to be over-reactive at first. What is more, through its stimulatory effects on certain organs and processes that

take place within the body, this kind of limited stress may even improve his resistance to disease.

There is nothing cruel about this treatment: it is only a man-made version of the natural way in which the puppy's mother will behave in a few days' time as she begins to wean him (see page 28). Having been handled in such a way, the puppy should be stroked gently before he is put back in the nest. Doing so will teach him that stroking follows stress, and will give him confidence to start turning to a person, not just to his mother, when he is unhappy.

Although the puppies may only be able to see a blurred image of their mother, they know who she is by her scent.

The importance of smell

The appearance of an object is often less interesting to a puppy (or to an older dog) than its odour. This is particularly true when eyesight is barely functional in the first weeks of life. It is a good idea to put objects that smell of important people – such as an unwashed T-shirt worn by the breeder, or even the owner-to-be – into the nest. This will help to prevent fearful reactions to those people later on, and should ease the stress that a puppy feels when moving to his new home.

A three-week-old Welsh corgi puppy is 14 cm (5½ in) long.

Week four

As he enters the fourth week of his life, the puppy is becoming fully aware of his surroundings for the first time. Many parts of his brain are now mature, although its separate components are not completely integrated. There is a marked increase in electrical activity in his brain, as huge numbers of microscopic nerves join up to produce one of the natural world's most sophisticated on-board computers.

Physical development

Despite all this brain activity, the puppy still needs a good deal of sleep. However, the second sleep centre in his brain is now working, and this allows him to experience shallow, peaceful sleep as well as the more 'twitchy' dreaming sleep to which he has been used. His body-temperature control will have improved, and the litter will tend to sleep side-by-side rather than in a heap, unless the surroundings are particularly cold.

WEANING

Towards the end of the fourth week, the process of weaning the litter of puppies on to solid food can begin. Initially, small amounts of very moist food will be all that they can manage. Any puppies who are lighter than the average for the litter – perhaps because they have not competed very effectively for the most productive nipples – should now be able to catch up.

A pet bitch may retain the wolf-type behaviour leading to weaning, which involves regurgitating partly digested food for the litter. Her puppies may even try to stimulate this by licking around her muzzle: this is another behaviour pattern seen in young wolves.

At four weeks old the puppies have grown very big. There is simply not enough room for them all to feed at the same time when their mother is lying down, so they will actively compete with each other for the best positions.

Through 'mouthing' each other while playing together (above), these puppies are beginning to learn how to control the power of their bite.

At the point of weaning, a bitch may need to consume four times more calories than she did before she was mated in order to provide her litter with sufficient food. However, given access to appropriate foods, puppies of large litters are unlikely to require much encouragement to fill up with solid rather than liquid fuel (left).

The puppy should now be able to stand, and will begin to urinate and defecate voluntarily, generally crawling out of the nest to do so.

Starting to play

As his vision and hearing improve, a puppy becomes increasingly aware of his litter mates, and starts to play and to interact with them. At first, this interaction consists largely of licking and chewing each other, and, as the puppies' needle-like canine teeth will have come through, such play can produce the odd yelp of pain.

This is the way in which puppies begin to learn how to control how hard they bite. It is a very important skill for use in later play, both with other dogs and with people. This is the beginning of what is known as socialization (see page 31).

Family ties

At this stage, a puppy's strongest ties are still firmly with his mother and his litter mates. If he is separated from either, he will soon begin to whimper and then to wail, even if all his physical needs are being met. He is becoming emotional!

At the end of the fourth week the puppies should be moved to a more 'public' location than before, although they will also need a covered space into which they can retreat. From now on they will benefit from a wide range of experiences. The longer puppies are isolated from different people and other animals, the more likely they are to become fearful of them.

A four-week-old Welsh corgi puppy is 18 cm (7¼ in) long.

Week five

By the beginning of his fifth week, the puppy will have become even more aware of his surroundings, and can clearly distinguish the shapes and movements of the objects around him. His eyes are no longer cloudy, and may already have changed from their initial greyish-blue to their adult colour.

The areas of the puppy's brain that are concerned with memory and learning have now enlarged considerably, and his spinal column is almost mature: this is a major breakthrough, as it allows the puppy to take his first faltering steps. Within a few days he is both walking and running, albeit in a somewhat uncoordinated fashion. His face has become much more expressive because he can move his ears, and his muzzle has lengthened.

Although five-week-old puppies are generally more interested in each other than in their mother, she will still play a vital role in helping her litter learn how to be dogs and to indulge in behaviour that is appropriate to their species.

Changing behaviour

The puppy's world now revolves largely around his litter mates rather than his mother, and playful fighting really begins in earnest. Chasing, pouncing, snapping, growling and snarling with bared teeth are all added to the repertoire of behaviour patterns.

A puppy may begin to practise prey-killing actions on toys, and some puppies will briefly guard toys from other members of the litter. Submissive gestures – such as rolling on the side and whining or licking at another puppy's jaw – also appear, but at this stage they are quite often ignored. By the time they are five weeks old, puppies may begin to invite each other to play by adopting certain specific body positions, such as the 'play-bow' and the raised paw (see page 37).

Gaining independence

The litter of boisterous puppies now behaves like a little 'pack', and can tolerate the absence of the mother. In fact, she will actively encourage the puppies to complete their weaning and become independent.

The bitch will tend to nurse the puppies standing up, and may walk away before they have drunk their fill. Between bouts of feeding she may snap her teeth as a warning to a puppy who tries to drink, and may even physically restrain him by pinning him down with her mouth. This is all quite natural behaviour: the bitch's instincts are telling her to save her strength for her next litter, now that this one can take solid food.

A five-week-old Welsh corgi puppy is 20 cm (8 in) long.

MAKING ACQUAINTANCES

A puppy, together with his brothers and sisters, should by the fifth and sixth weeks of his life be experiencing regular contact with a number of people of different ages, sexes, appearance and odour, as well as with other animals. Puppies with only limited experience of a wide range of people up to this point can still be socialized, even though they may be initially fearful, but isolation beyond this time can lead to problems in the long term.

Week six

Although the socialization phase spans the period between the fourth and twelfth weeks of a puppy's life, it is probably during the sixth week that he is most susceptible to new experiences. His willingness to approach novel objects, people and animals is at its peak, and his breeder should take advantage of this by presenting the puppy with a wide variety of experiences within a stable and safe environment.

The puppy should now be introduced to a range of different people, including men and children. Many puppies encounter only women during their first eight weeks, and can subsequently remain fearful of humans of a different sex or age. The litter should be provided with an indoor playpen containing toys with which the puppies can play on their own, and with which they can play games with people. Dog-friendly cats can also be introduced at this age.

What is socialization?

This term is the current buzz word of the dog world, but it is often wrongly used. From a scientific point of view, it has two meanings. The first relates to the positive behavioural adjustments that a puppy makes during acclimatization to other dogs, other animals and people. The second covers the ways in which

By the sixth week, the puppies are very boisterous. Their play is actually a more serious business than you might imagine, as it helps them to learn all kinds of interactive skills.

A six-week-old Welsh corgi puppy is 23 cm (9¼ in) long.

owners can promote this process of familiarization. All mammals go through a form of socialization when they are young. What is unusual, or perhaps special, about a puppy is that he seems naturally capable of socializing with several species of animal – such as humans, cats and other dogs – at once.

Why is socialization important?

For a puppy, successful socialization with his own kind depends upon continued contact with other dogs. This is why it is unwise to re-home a puppy before he is seven weeks old, even though he is independent of his mother by the age of six weeks. Such a puppy will have difficulty in relating to other dogs: he may behave aggressively towards them, and may display sexual behaviour towards people. Quite simply, he will turn into a dog who does not realize he is a dog!

Fun and games

Although six-week-old puppies should approach people fearlessly and spontaneously, they are still bound up in the social world of their litter mates.

Play becomes more complex, as do invitations to play. A playful puppy may approach another in an exaggerated, 'bouncy' manner: an amusing behaviour pattern that works well on humans too. The 'approach-withdrawal' tactic involves skulking up to another puppy and then darting away in the hope of being chased. This type of play develops communication skills, and the puppy's ability to judge the 'mood' of other dogs.

Weeks seven and eight

By the start of the seventh week of life, the explosive development of a very young puppy is coming to an end. He can now keep his body temperature stable at around 38.6°C (101.5°F), which is the same as that of an adult dog. The growth of his brain has slowed to that of the rest of his body, his hearing is fully developed and he has acquired full visual abilities.

New experiences

The socialization phase has now peaked. Puppies who have been raised in restricted environments are likely to be over-exploratory, difficult to train and fearful of people and/or other dogs. However, those who have received the recommended encounters since the fourth week can now have their experiences widened further.

This can be done by offering the puppies a larger play area that includes objects to explore and in which they can play, such as sections of pipe, flower pots and cardboard boxes, as well as toys. The play area should also contain a variety of substrates such as concrete, gravel, earth, grass, floor tiles and carpet. Sadly, many puppies must start their lives believing that the world is paved with newspaper!

APTITUDE-TESTING

In some places, aptitude tests are now carried out on puppies at about seven weeks of age, and can provide valuable information about a puppy's temperament that will help when it comes to matching him to an appropriate owner. For example, a highly intelligent, outgoing individual may be most suitable for complex training, whereas a more submissive, placid puppy is likely to be less of a handful for an elderly owner.

A seven-week-old puppy should live in a stimulating environment. Being so inquisitive, puppies of this age need proper supervision to ensure that they do not get into trouble.

These aptitude tests are still in their infancy, and are currently being tested scientifically to see whether they can predict how a puppy will behave when he is older.

Fearfulness

At present, fearfulness is the only consistent aspect found to persist from puppy- to adulthood. What this shows is that a puppy's character is not fully formed at the age of seven or eight weeks, and that a new owner can do much to alter it in the following weeks.

Sibling rivalries

The temperament of a puppy in a litter may be greatly affected by his brothers and sisters. For instance, once separated from a very bossy, intimidating litter mate, a submissive puppy may quickly gain in confidence. Equally, the behaviour of the bossy puppy may change rapidly once he meets older, more dominant dogs.

A seven-week-old Welsh corgi puppy is 26 cm (10½ in) long.

PERSONAL HYGIENE

Good care as well as clean living conditions are important factors in determining a young puppy's behaviour as he grows older. Given the opportunity, a puppy of seven or eight weeks old will select for himself the places in which he urinates and defecates.

Unfortunately, some puppies are brought up in unhygienic environments where they become habituated to the smell of faeces. Such puppies are generally much more difficult to house-train, and may even develop coprophagia (faeces eating) later in life.

By eight weeks of age (above) it is time for most puppies to say goodbye to their mother and litter mates. Despite the very close bonds between them, most puppies will adjust quickly to a new environment if the transition is handled sensitively by all those concerned.

An eight-week-old Welsh corgi puppy is 30 cm (12 in) long.

From eight weeks to one year

The development of a puppy once he has reached the normal age for re-homing (see page 68) has not been studied in such great depth as the complex mental and physical changes that he undergoes during the first eight weeks of his life. There is little doubt, however, that a puppy's experiences from eight weeks onwards have a significant influence on his character and his disposition as an adult dog.

Physical progress

The young puppy's physical development continues throughout the weeks after he has moved in with his new owners. By the time he is 12 weeks old he has complete control over both urination and defecation, and should be well on the way to being successfully toilet-trained (see pages 74–7).

The puppy's co-ordination and movement skills develop and improve over an extended period of time as his brain continues to grow. His adult, permanent teeth begin to appear when he is about 17 weeks old, and his smaller puppy teeth (known as 'deciduous' teeth) will have all been shed – and often swallowed – by the time he is seven months old.

At this stage, a puppy of a medium-sized breed will be about two-thirds of his full adult size.

Sexual behaviour

Sexually orientated behaviour may start as early as eight weeks of age, when some male puppies begin to engage in mounting, clasping and pelvic thrusting as part of their play behaviour. Certain females may also behave in this way when trying to dominate other puppies. Male dogs generally show sexual interest in females from four months onwards, although females are likely to reject such advances until their first heat at about seven months of age (see pages 122–3).

FROM EIGHT WEEKS TO SIX MONTHS

During this period, a puppy will learn a great deal about his environment, and about the people and animals within it. Although puppies of most breeds have an attention span that is too short for them to be taught complex tasks, all puppies should now be capable of learning simple commands. Many puppies can in fact be successfully taught the re-call command (see page 82) when they are just eight weeks old.

Playing with an older dog – in this case, a one-year-old from the same family – is an important learning experience for these eight-week-old puppies.

THE 'FEAR/AVOIDANCE' PERIOD

Before the socialization phase ends at about 12 weeks, a puppy may go through a period of mild fearfulness, shyness and deliberate avoidance of new experiences, until he enters the juvenile phase at about 13 weeks.

This is a natural process that helps to prevent the young but increasingly independent puppy from becoming accidentally socialized to other, inappropriate species, or to others of his own kind who are not members of his immediate family.

This fear/avoidance period occurs when a puppy is about eight to 10 weeks old, and is much less severe than in wild mammals. Many owners do not even notice that it is happening, but, given that it occurs at the same time or soon after most puppies move to their new homes, it is a wise precaution to make this period as stress-free for the puppy as possible.

Broadening horizons

Some experts believe that there is a distinct period of environmental learning that takes place from about 12 to 25 weeks, during which a puppy seeks a broader range of experiences beyond his immediate family.

This is the time at which the puppy will benefit greatly from being taken by his owner to socialization classes or a 'puppy playgroup' (see page 80). Ideally, all puppies should attend such gatherings as soon as they have been fully vaccinated (see page 121), and if at all possible before they are 14 weeks old.

Continued exposure to other dogs through such means during the first six months of life is vital, and will guard against a puppy becoming fearful of or aggressive towards his own kind.

By regularly weighing a puppy as he develops physically, a vet or veterinary nurse can compare his growth rate with the expected 'growth curve' for that particular breed. Small dogs reach their adult weights sooner than the larger breeds. For instance, a cairn terrier is considered to be fully grown at the age of about seven months, whereas an Irish wolfhound may still be growing a little at his first birthday. A cross-bred puppy will have a growth curve that is unique to him.

Early learning

A well-adjusted young dog will have been exposed to all kinds of people, other animals and environments from an early age. However, because a puppy is so eager to learn during the first six months of his life, it is very important that his owner always reinforces the correct responses when new situations arise.

In particular, stroking, patting, cuddling or any other attentive behaviour on the part of an owner, immediately following a fearful or aggressive response by a puppy, will only serve to ensure that the same inappropriate response is repeated when the situation occurs the next time. Praise should always be reserved for neutral or positive responses by a puppy to new experiences (see page 88).

FROM SIX MONTHS TO ONE YEAR

Recent research indicates that, if a puppy is re-homed during this period, he is likely to develop undesirable behaviour – such as howling, barking, destructive behaviour or toileting in the house – when left alone.

This suggests that it is at this age that a puppy develops strong attachments to specific people and places, and that he will become distressed if these are broken in any way. It is important that a puppy learns from a young age that, when he is left by himself, his owner will always return (see pages 94–5).

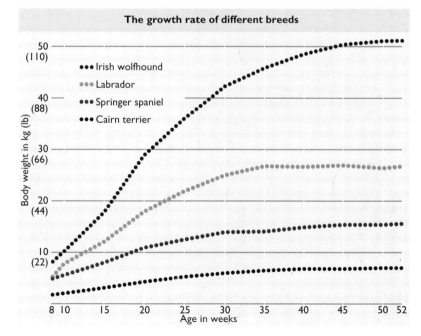

The growth rate of different breeds

- ••• Irish wolfhound
- ••• Labrador
- ••• Springer spaniel
- ••• Cairn terrier

Body weight in kg (lb)

50 (110)
40 (88)
30 (66)
20 (44)
10 (22)

8 10   15   20   25   30   35   40   45   50 52

Age in weeks

Preparing for a new puppy

Taking on a new puppy is a major commitment, and you will need to prepare well for this new addition to your family. You will find advice here on picking the perfect puppy to ensure a successful relationship, as well as on important practical considerations such as feeding – and making your home puppy-proof.

Understanding dogs

There may soon be a puppy in your life. By learning in advance something of the body language and communication methods used by dogs, you should avoid any unnecessary and frustrating communication crises when he comes to live with you. In time, you should become more and more sensitive to his feelings, and better able to adapt the way that you behave in his company, in order to make yourself simpler for him to understand. You will then find it much easier to control and to train your puppy properly.

Talking in the wild

For wolves, being able to communicate effectively is essential for survival. Over thousands of years, they have perfected a way of 'talking' to each other using a combination of scent marks, body postures and behaviour patterns, as well as a few specific sounds.

Using these methods, wolves can communicate over long distances as well as face-to-face, and they can even leave each other messages (see page 38).

Communication between dogs

To varying degrees, pet dogs share the communication abilities of their wild ancestors. Even a young puppy rapidly learns the essentials of dog body language through playing with his brothers and sisters, and by interacting with his mother. As he grows older, he should be allowed to practise and perfect these skills through regular contact with other dogs.

When making friends with a puppy, do not lunge forwards to stroke or cuddle him, but get down to his level and let the puppy explore you in his own time.

Human relationships

If a puppy is to form good and lasting relationships with his human companions, he must learn something about the methods that we use to communicate.

Fortunately, all dogs are gifted with remarkable observation skills and an amazing ability to learn quickly, and even young puppies are soon able to make sense of us despite the fact that what we actually say is meaningless to them. In fact, if dogs were not so talented, it is doubtful that they would ever have got on so well with people. However, communication breakdowns between dogs and people do arise – all too often as a result of simple misunderstandings.

BODY LANGUAGE

By adopting certain postures, facial expressions and behaviours, many animals – including ourselves – communicate their moods to others of their kind. Smiling, waving, hand-shaking and kissing are all elements of human body language that do not normally require supplementation with words. But because we rely so heavily on the written and spoken word to communicate, we are not very good at picking up more subtle body-language signals.

Dogs are different: they use body language as one of their main methods of communication, and are programmed from birth to be highly skilled observers of the way other animals look and behave.

Body-language signals

The following are just a few excerpts from the dog body-language phrasebook.

Ears pricked forwards • I may just be interested in something, but I may be threatening you.

Ears pulled backwards • I am feeling intimidated.

Eyes in a direct stare • I may be threatening you, but I may be calm and simply quizzical.

Eyes looking away • I feel intimidated.

Hackles raised • I am highly aroused. I may just be excited, but I could easily be feeling aggressive.

Twitching lips • I am feeling aggressive.

Lips pulled back, exposing teeth • If I am snarling then I am giving you a final warning. I am threatening you and I am aggressive.

Tail held high • I am alert.

Tail held low • I am a little unsure of how I feel.

Tail low and wagging • I am a little anxious and nervous, and I feel that you could intimidate me.

Tail tucked between legs • I am frightened.

Tail high and wagging • I am happy, but I may also be rather confused.

Standing tall at full height • I am strong, intimidating and impressive.

Cowering/crouching with head held low • I am being submissive towards you, or I am frightened.

Rolled over on side • I am being incredibly servile; in fact so servile that I may lose control of my bladder!

By raising one paw, a puppy indicates his desire to play. He may adopt the same posture when begging for food or a favourite toy.

A wagging tail, a relaxed facial expression and pricked ears are all clear signs of a puppy who is happy and alert.

An aggressive and angry puppy stands erect with his tail held high and his hackles raised. He stares directly at the object of his anger, and snarls and growls.

A frightened puppy tucks his tail firmly between his legs, cowers towards the ground and holds his ears pinned back against the side of his head.

SCENT MESSAGES

Dogs have a far keener sense of smell than humans. When a dog and his owner first encounter a new environment, they will each perceive it in different ways: the owner will be interested in the visual impact of the surroundings, while the dog will be much more interested in their scents, many of which will go totally unnoticed by his human companion.

Territory-marking

The advantage of scent messages is that they last a long time in the environment, and do not require the dogs that produced them to be present in order for the messages to be understood.

Wolves mark the boundaries of their territories by leaving scent clues via their urine, faeces and other body scents. Faeces may not be an important communication tool for pet dogs, but urine is used very frequently. When out and about in places that many dogs visit, male dogs will normally 'urine-mark' by cocking a leg and spraying a small volume of urine on to selected objects. The same structures are often overmarked by many other male dogs. Bitches also urine-mark: most will squat to do so, but some will occasionally cock a hindleg in the same way as males.

What does urine-marking mean?

Quite what information dogs leave behind when they urine-mark is a matter of debate, but there is no doubt that the marks provide clues as to the dogs' sex, size and of course presence. The strength of the scent may give some indication of when they were there.

Other forms of marking

Many male dogs and some bitches also scratch the ground and kick out debris and vegetation with their hindlegs after defecating. Doing so may give a visual message to other dogs of the individual's presence, or may provide further smell messages from body scents produced by the foot pads and the skin between the toes. No-one knows for sure.

BARKS, GROWLS, WHINES AND HOWLS

Despite their heavy reliance on non-vocal forms of communication, dogs are not silent animals. They bark, growl, whine and howl, and young puppies often grunt as a sign of contentment. Barking is a peculiarity of tame dogs, being little used by dogs in the wild. A dog may bark when defending his territory, while playing, as a greeting, or as a call for attention. Growls are threat signals. A dog may whine and whimper to show that he is behaving submissively, or that he is in pain, anxious, unhappy or attention-seeking. Wolves howl to seek contact with others and to call the pack together for hunting; pet dogs who howl are probably lonely and in need of company.

Personal scent

A dog's unique scent is produced by special areas of skin on his face, tail and around his anus and genitals. All dogs have a pair of anal sacs that store body secretions. Occasionally dogs can have problems with these sacs, which may require manual emptying by a vet. Ask anyone who has had to empty them, and you will discover that the secretions that they contain are extremely pungent even to the human nose. Exactly how the sacs are used is not clear, but they do not play a part in creating a dog's personal scent.

The great importance of personal odour in dog communication is most obvious when two dogs meet as strangers to each other. After a cautious approach, most of the time that they spend at close quarters is occupied by sniffing at each other's bodies. Dogs and bitches then tend to behave differently: no matter what the sex of the other dog, females often concentrate on the head, whereas males almost always sniff the region around the anus and genitals.

INTERACTING WITH DOGS

At first, our body language and vocal communications must seem very strange to dogs. For instance, when we pull back our lips and reveal our teeth we are generally happy, but this expression on a dog's face is a display of aggression. However, as puppies, dogs soon learn the meanings of the ways humans look, sound and behave in particular situations.

Using body language

When interacting with a puppy, do not concentrate just on what he is doing, but think about how you are behaving, what you are saying and the tone of your voice. Are you making yourself easy to understand, or are you giving out confusing signals?

For example, if your puppy has shredded a towel, you will be unhappy with him. If you respond by touching him to get his attention and then say: 'You naughty dog – now you'll just have to wait for your dinner', the chances are that his tail will start wagging.

Look at your behaviour from his point of view. He may have destroyed the towel because he was lonely. As soon as you came back, you touched him and spoke to him – exactly what he wanted you to do. And, of all the words you used, 'dinner' was probably the only one with any meaning! If your puppy fails to grasp a message, try to change the way that you deliver it.

PUPPY-HANDLING TIPS

• When approaching a timid puppy, avoid towering above him, staring into his eyes or moving quickly towards him with your arms outstretched. He is likely to back away from apprehension. Instead, get down to his level and then remain still.

• Offer a hand for the puppy to come and inspect. Rather than looking into his eyes as he comes towards you, focus on another part of his body, such as his tail.

• Dogs always prefer to know their social position. Encouraging submissive behaviour in a puppy – such as by making him roll over to expose his belly – will reinforce his perception that humans are pack leaders, and that he should behave submissively towards them.

• Puppies become confused and will often be more assertive if they are not treated consistently by all those with whom they live. Children should be encouraged to learn the basic rules, and everyone must stick to them.

• Whether stroking a puppy, grooming him, drying his feet, bathing him, cleaning his teeth, giving him medicines or interacting with him in any other way, always behave calmly and confidently towards him. A friendly but firm approach should tell a puppy that he has nothing to fear or to fight against.

• When handling a puppy who is struggling – even playfully – avoid letting him go until he is calm. If he is allowed to believe that struggling results in his release, he will quickly become difficult to handle.

• Avoid being over-rough or aggressive when playing with a puppy, as this may encourage him to engage in battles of strength with people in general.

• When talking directly to a puppy, always be sure to speak concisely and clearly.

• Puppies trained to hand signals as well as to verbal commands are often more responsive to their owners.

By regularly asking her puppy to roll over, this young owner is encouraging the puppy to behave submissively towards her. In this way, she will help to ensure that both her authority and her higher status in the family are respected.

What makes a good owner?

No matter how much you may love dogs, affection alone will not keep a puppy fit and healthy. What you need is commitment, and plenty of it. If you take on a new puppy, you will be responsible most of the time for what he does, when he does it and where he goes to do it. He will be dependent on you, and it will be your responsibility to nourish, protect and educate him.

The following points and questions will help you to decide whether you have what it takes to be a good and conscientious dog-owner.

Preparing your home

Your house, garden and car will need to be adapted to accommodate your new puppy. There will be a number of dog-care items to buy, some of which will be expensive (see pages 52–3). You may need to fence your garden, or to cover your pond. It will all cost money. Do you have the budget to spend? Your puppy

Feeding your puppy will involve more than just preparing his food: you will need to weigh him regularly to check on his progress.

must also be able to go to the toilet at home, so you will need to dedicate a part of your garden solely for this purpose (see page 50). Do you have the space?

Food

Your puppy will have special dietary requirements, and you will need to think very carefully about how to satisfy them (see pages 54–67). The cost of buying good-quality food is likely to be the single largest item in your dog-care budget. Can you afford this?

Education

Dogs are born with the instincts of free-living pack animals, and your puppy will need help to adjust to your lifestyle. When you collect him at around eight weeks old, he should already have learned a great deal about the world, but he will still need to learn what is acceptable behaviour and what is not. Whether or not he turns into a well-adjusted canine member of human society is up to you (see pages 80–7). Do you have the time and patience to train and socialize him properly?

Exercise

All dogs require physical and mental exercise in order to stay fit and healthy (see pages 90–3). Many working parents are amazed at how difficult it is to find time for their children. Are you prepared to build play and exercise time for your puppy into your schedule? How do you feel about walks in the pouring rain?

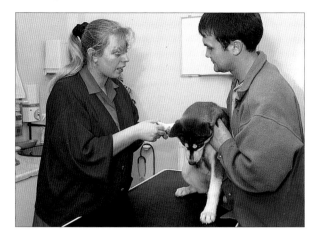

If your puppy is ill or injured, you could face unexpected medical costs. If this is likely to cause financial difficulties, you should consider health insurance for him (see page 107).

Healthcare

Dogs need regular vaccinations, parasite control, dental care and grooming. Some of these tasks you can undertake at home yourself; others will need to be carried out by your vet or a veterinary nurse (see page 104–5). Accidents and illness can happen at any time, and some long-term problems may need years of treatment. Can you cope with the emotional and financial strain of sudden, major medical care? Are you prepared to nurse your puppy when he is sick?

Holidays

Will you always take your puppy on holiday with you (see pages 98–9)? If not, what will you do with him?

Finances

You may be able to afford to keep a dog now, but what if your circumstances suddenly change? Are you prepared to make sacrifices elsewhere in your life?

Your family

Even if you plan to be entirely responsible for the care of your new puppy, he will still interact with all the members of your family, and will see them as part of his pack. Does everyone in your house like dogs as much as you do? Inevitably, especially while learning the rules, your puppy will damage your property. He may chew up someone's favourite shoes, unearth prize plants, go to the toilet on your Persian rug and scratch the car upholstery. He may do all these things and more. How will you and your family react?

Will you all accept with good humour odd hairs in your food when your puppy is moulting? What about muddy paw prints on your clothes and the carpet when he dashes in from a walk and has a mad half-hour racing around your living-room? Will anyone in your house consider these predictable events to be major disasters? If so, your puppy's life could be made a misery. If you invite him in, you must welcome him wholeheartedly, muddy paws and all.

Your work

How will your employers react to your new sidekick? Have you broached the subject of taking your puppy to work with you? Your colleagues may put up with your puppy at first, but their dislike of him or his habits could put a serious strain on your personal and professional relationships later on. If you cannot take your puppy to work, what will you do with him?

Other people

Many habits of dogs, such as barking, are considered a nuisance by most other dog-owners and non-dog-owners alike. What will your neighbours think about you owning a puppy? Are you prepared to prevent him from fouling in public? If he does so by accident, are you willing to clean up after him?

Legal responsibilities

As a dog-owner you may have to obey national dog-licensing laws, and you will be legally responsible for your puppy's health and welfare (see page 101). Are you prepared to comply with these laws?

Thinking ahead

Your puppy may live for over 10 years. How might your life change in that time? If you are single, might you live with someone else? What will happen if you have to move house, possibly abroad? If you have children, how will your dog fit in? Consider events such as sudden illness, disability or death. What will happen to your dog? You should be prepared to make provision for him, just as you would for your family. Your responsibility to him is for life – his, not yours.

WARNING

Some people are seriously allergic to dogs. If you think that you or a member of your family may react badly to the presence of a dog in the house, talk to your doctor before taking any steps to obtain a puppy.

Making the right choice

Your next important task is to decide what sort of puppy would suit you best. Your aim here should be to create a shortlist of possible dog breeds or types that you can investigate in greater detail, in order to reach a final decision. Now is also the time to think about your future puppy's sex, and whether you would like a young or an older puppy.

There are several hundred breeds of dog, and countless 'styles' of cross-bred or mongrel dogs, from which to choose. Many people are drawn to a breed because it is familiar, or simply because they like the look of it, but picking a breed solely on the basis that some individuals are appealing can be a big mistake.

What type of puppy will suit you?

Understanding the behavioural differences between certain breeds is extremely important, as human-dog relationships regularly break down when dogs of a particular mentality are expected to live a lifestyle to which they are unsuited. If you are already attracted to a breed because of its looks, try to put aside those feelings for now. Your dog's temperament will be a great deal more significant in the long run.

It is extremely important to identify the kind of dog that will fit your personality and lifestyle. For instance, you will have less chance of a fruitful relationship with a typically territorial and aggressive breed if you have a busy social life and lots of dog-owning friends!

SELF-ASSESSMENT

The first step in choosing the right puppy is to make a thorough and objective assessment of yourself and the other members of your family.

Your personality

If you believe in strict discipline and tend to have a stentorian tone of voice, a puppy of one of the more sensitive breeds would not suit you. He might simply over-react, and become so submissive that he would be far from a happy and confident companion.

Neither would you get on very well with a puppy of a breed known for its independent disposition, as you would find his natural stubbornness extremely infuriating. But you and a manageable yet confident, outgoing type of dog – such as a boxer – may very well end up the best of friends.

Similarly, if you are liberal in your outlook and do not wish to have a dog who will need firm handling,

a puppy of a highly independent breed could be a recipe for disaster. A breed such as a Cavalier King Charles spaniel would be much more appropriate.

Your family

Your puppy will have to interact with all the members of your family. He should be especially well-suited to the person with whom he will spend most time, but he must also be well-matched to his other co-habitees.

Practicalities

How much and what kind of exercise will you be able to give your puppy? This will depend on many factors, such as where you live, the size of your house and garden and your physical abilities.

You should also identify what it is that you want from the relationship. In short, why do you want a dog at all? What will be his main function in life? Will he be a companion for adults, or also a playmate for children? Will he be expected to work, for instance on hunting trips? Do you want him to participate in a dog hobby, such as agility or obedience work?

Be honest

Objectivity at this stage is essential: if you make a critical assessment now, you will be doing all you can to avoid frustration later on. Sadly, many dogs are re-homed or destroyed every year because of behavioural problems resulting from a mismatch of personalities.

After this rigorous self-assessment, you should have a character profile of the sort of dog that would suit you best. Only then can you begin to create a shortlist of breeds to match that description.

BREED CHARACTERISTICS

Traditionally, different breeds of dog have always been grouped by their intended vocations. There are the hounds, including the beagle and the greyhound; the herding dogs, such as the collie and the corgi; the guard breeds, including the rottweiler and the Pyrenean and Bernese mountain dogs; the sporting breeds, such as the spaniel and the retriever; and, of course, the terriers. Finally, there is a small group of dogs, such as the Cavalier King Charles spaniel, whose primary function has been that of companionship. The breeds in this last group usually make excellent family pets, as they have been bred for generations to be non-aggressive, fun-loving and affectionate animals.

Dogs have been bred by man for many purposes, and the original function of a breed gives a strong indication of the characteristics that it is likely to show. The following types of dog are both good examples.

The terriers

The stocky West Highland white terrier, the diminutive Yorkshire terrier, the aristocratic Bedlington terrier and even the oddly shaped dachshund were all originally bred as killers. Sent after rats, badgers or foxes, all these dogs earned their keep by fighting for their lives underground. Is it really surprising, then, that they are considered plucky, spirited animals who believe they are as big as Great Danes and twice as strong? Or that they tend to be independent, alert characters with a reputation for being snappy? After all, in the depths of a foxhole, an 'attack first – ask questions later' policy is most likely to keep you in one piece.

This independent streak means that, although the terriers are perfectly trainable, it can be difficult to motivate them to listen to you.

The working breeds

Working breeds, such as the border collie and springer spaniel, need plenty of mental stimulation and a great deal of training: this may be obedience work or agility, or something more informal. But a working dog who is not given specific tasks to perform will soon start to create his own amusement, and his idea of fun may not promote a happy relationship with his owner.

The working breeds are very popular as pets, but the fact that they make up a large proportion of a behaviour counsellor's workload shows that they are often taken on by the wrong people. Yet, when treated appropriately, they are extremely rewarding creatures.

Hundreds of pure- and cross-bred dogs are available, of which just a few popular breeds and types are shown below. (Clockwise from top left) mongrel, Welsh corgi, Pekinese, English setter, German shepherd, French bulldog, mongrel, golden retriever, wire-haired dachshund, Cavalier King Charles spaniel, cross-bred springer spaniel, basset hound.

Breed-behaviour profiles

The following classifications of just some of the most popular dog breeds have been taken from the results of a study at the University of Southampton in the UK.

This information is included here to help to direct your further research: it is not a complete guide to the expected character of all dog breeds, and there will be individual dogs who do not conform to the suggested behaviour for their breed. However, the profiles are based on the opinions of 112 veterinary surgeons as well as 56 other dog-care professionals, so they should be taken seriously.

If you live outside the UK, try to find out whether similar studies have been carried out in your country: the results may be different from those outlined here.

Group one

Examples of breeds
Rottweiler, German shepherd (right).

Typical characteristics
These breeds are intelligent, but require a firm hand to keep them under control. They tend to be faithful and obedient to their owners and other members of the household, but do not accept strangers easily. They are not particularly playful.

Breeds in this category display all the qualities required for their original function, which was primarily that of guarding. They are 'slow to fire', assessing a situation fully before showing aggression. However, they do not back off easily and will defend to the death.

Behavioural summary
High aggression, average reactivity, low immaturity.

Conclusion
Unsuitable as family pets.

Group two

Examples of breeds
British bulldog, chow chow (right).

Typical characteristics
The bulldog was bred originally as a sturdy fighting dog, and the chow chow as a hunting and watch dog.

Both of these breeds are strong-willed, and have highly independent characters. Over time, they tend to form very strong loyalties and attachments to the other members – both human and animal – of their immediate group. These dogs display a general assertiveness and independence, combined with a not particularly playful attitude to life.

Behavioural summary
Average aggression, low reactivity, low immaturity.

Conclusion
Unsuitable as family pets.

Group three

Examples of breeds
King Charles spaniel, Cavalier King Charles spaniel (right).

Typical characteristics
The breeds represented in this group are affectionate dogs, who take a great deal of interest in their surroundings and make good watch dogs. They are less demanding than the breeds in Group eight, but they will willingly join in the activities taking place around them. This characteristic, combined with their friendly natures, makes these breeds ideal pets for families who do not have the space or time to cope with the boisterous nature of the springer spaniels and retrievers.

Behavioural summary
Low aggression, high reactivity, low immaturity.

Conclusion
Excellent pets, suitable for almost any type of owner.

Group four

Examples of breeds
Greyhound, whippet, basset hound (right).

Typical characteristics
These dogs tend to be fairly self-willed and affectionate creatures. They are not the easiest of groups to train, as they require a great deal of motivating and can be rather single-minded. They make delightful pets for owners who do not demand too much from a dog other than his company and affection.

Unlike the members of Group seven, this group scores low on aggression, and the smaller members such as the whippet would be excellent companions for elderly owners who are looking for a relaxed relationship with a dog.

Behavioural summary
Low aggression, low reactivity, low immaturity.

Conclusion
Good for quieter owners.

Group five

Examples of breeds
Old English sheepdog, samoyed, rough collie, standard poodle (right).

Typical characteristics
This is a difficult group to summarize, as it includes a mixed collection of breeds that do not fall clearly into any of the other categories described here. In general, dogs in this group do not make ideal family pets.

Any prospective owner should read up on the original function and characteristics of breeds in this group. For instance, the samoyed was used as a sled dog and beast of burden. Lively and intelligent, it requires a lot of exercise, and is not particularly trainable. By contrast, the standard poodle was originally a gun dog and is a far more biddable creature. This breed appreciates human company, and also enjoys and needs a great deal of mental stimulation.

Behavioural summary
Average aggression, average reactivity, average immaturity.

Conclusion
Generally, not a group comprising breeds that would make good family pets.

Group six

Examples of breeds
Jack Russell, cairn terrier, West Highland white terrier, fox terrier, corgi (right).

Typical characteristics
Bred originally to eradicate vermin, the terriers rate highly on the aggression quotient. Unlike the breeds of Group one, they are very playful, and particularly enjoy games with squeaky and tug toys. These 'killing' games reflect the emphasis in their selection for their fighting ability or, with the corgi, the similar need to be able to dart in behind cattle and egg them on with a quick nip.

These dogs must be taught appropriate play and how to control their 'play-bite', particularly in the presence of children.

Although trainable, the members of this group may require considerable motivation to divert their attention from the more interesting occupation of chasing squirrels (or joggers). They can be fairly noisy dogs, and very active as they react to passers-by or noises outdoors.

Behavioural summary
High aggression, average reactivity, high immaturity.

Conclusion
Unsuitable as family pets, especially in families with young children.

Group seven

Examples of breeds
Yorkshire terrier, toy poodle, chihuahua (right).

Typical characteristics
The diminutive stature of these dogs makes them extremely popular, but their size can be misleading. These dogs are very bright, and must be trained to be obedient. In addition, as with all breeds, they need to be socialized to different people and animals (see page 31), or they can become snappy – a trait that would not be tolerated in a larger breed.

The size of these breeds also means that they are not suitable for families with young children. During play, children often unintentionally cause pain, which can lead to aggression on the part of the dog. These are also not particularly playful dogs, and are not friendly to everybody.

As with any breed, a prospective owner should look back to these dogs' original function to gain an idea of their characters: even the tiny Yorkie is actually a deadly ratter at heart.

Behavioural summary
Average aggression, high reactivity, low immaturity.

Conclusion
Not suited to families with young children.

Group eight

Examples of breeds
English setter, Irish setter, springer spaniel, golden retriever (right).

Typical characteristics
This group is characterized by a happy-go-lucky outlook on life. Given appropriate training and socialization (see page 31), they are everybody's friends and assume that all the world wants to play. The breeds listed here were all originally gun dogs, bred to be robust in their travels through the undergrowth, mud and streams of the countryside, as well as willing and obedient hunting partners.
These dogs make wonderful companions, are full of fun and are always willing to accompany their owners on any adventure. However, their gun-dog instincts mean that they will pick up and carry all sorts of objects. Teaching the 'drop' in a positive manner right from the start will prevent any problems later. All too often, when in possession of an object, these breeds show an aggression that has developed purely because their owners used confrontational techniques to retrieve objects when the dogs were puppies.

Behavioural summary
Low aggression, average reactivity, high immaturity.

Conclusion
Excellent family pets.

GOOD LOOKS

There is no doubt at all that, when it comes to canine appearance, beauty is in the eye of the beholder. When you have made all the really important decisions, you can think about your future puppy's looks, but there are still a few practical considerations.

For instance, all dogs need grooming, but those with long hair need more attention than their shorter-coated relatives to keep their coats in top condition. It will also come as no surprise that – in general – dogs with big bodies need big beds, big bowls and owners with bigger bank balances. And the more unnatural a dog looks, the more likely he will be to require medical attention. For example, dogs with flat faces are prone to breathing difficulties; those with bulging eyes often injure them. All such factors should play a part in your final choice.

OTHER CONSIDERATIONS

Just from the examples given on the previous pages, it should be obvious that a comprehensive study of the different breeds is essential if you are to identify the right kind of puppy for you and your family.

Once you have completed your research on this subject, and have picked out the breed of puppy that you think you would like, you will need to think about the following aspects.

One puppy or two?

If you are concerned about the amount of time that your puppy will spend alone, you may consider obtaining two puppies. However, this is not a valid solution to your concern, and may lead to serious problems. For instance, training two puppies is more difficult than teaching one. The puppies will also bond with each other more strongly at first than they will with you, but, as they grow older, they may compete for the position of top dog (especially if they are male).

If you wish to have two dogs, wait until the first is over one year old. By that age, he should be well-trained and have developed a strong relationship with you. You will then be able to concentrate on the new puppy, as you will have to put in a lot of time and effort in order to prevent him from bonding with your older dog rather than with you.

Male or female?

As a rule, bitches are more manageable and easier to train than males. They are also more submissive, and so are less likely to attempt to climb the social ladder and challenge the authority of their owners.

Unspayed bitches may have 'mood' swings when they are in heat, as well as during pseudo-pregnancy (see pages 122–3). Males tend to be more boisterous and independent, and are also more challenging to train. Uncastrated males tend to roam if not restricted, and are more likely to be aggressive towards other male dogs. Whichever sex you decide upon, it is advisable to have your dog neutered if you do not intend to use him or her for breeding purposes.

Pure or mixed breed?

Pure-bred • The advantage of choosing a pure-bred puppy is that you will have a good idea of how big he will grow, and what his behavioural traits will be. However, many people – including myself – prefer cross-bred dogs and mongrels.

Cross-bred • A puppy is described as a cross-bred dog if both his parents were pure breeds, but of different types. In this case, knowing who the parents are will give you some idea as to the kind of dog he will become. However, the mysteries of genetics are such that there are no guarantees that a puppy will grow up to resemble one parent more than the other.

Mongrel • A puppy may be called a mongrel if one or both of his parents were cross-breds or mongrels themselves. In this case, it will be even harder to predict what the puppy will look like or what kind of character he will have when he is fully grown.

Do not be under the illusion that pure-bred dogs are 'better' than cross-breds and mongrels. As far as health is concerned exactly the reverse is in fact the rule, as many pure-bred dogs are prone to specific diseases that are less often seen in other types of dog. The choice is yours, but, no matter what kind of dog you eventually decide upon, you should never obtain a puppy without having met and liked his mother, and if possible his father (see pages 48–9).

Young or old?

The best age to adopt a puppy is when he is seven to eight weeks old (see page 68), but you may wish to consider taking on an older puppy. A well-socialized, well-trained puppy of six to 12 months will make a wonderful pet for the right person, but choosing an older puppy is no simpler than selecting a younger one. You will have to do much the same research, but some of it may be difficult or impossible to carry out: for instance, if the puppy is at a rescue centre. Such dogs are usually best-suited to experienced owners.

In general, puppies who are re-homed when older are more prone to exhibiting behavioural problems when left alone (see page 35). On the other hand, although you will have greater control over the early development of a young puppy, you will also have the work that caring for and training a youngster entails.

In my opinion, taking on a young puppy is the best option for most first-time owners, as it is both fun and highly educational to witness the transformation of a puppy into an adult dog.

Even if it takes you several weeks, you should spend the necessary time to research all the options available when choosing your puppy. Having identified the kind of dog that is best-suited to your lifestyle, you will be much more likely to enjoy a happy and rewarding relationship with your canine companion over the years ahead.

Finding a puppy

Once you have settled on the type of puppy that you would like, you can start looking for possible places from which to obtain one. If you have decided that you would like a pure-bred puppy from a litter, your first task should be to find the right breeding bitch: in appearance – and, more importantly, in temperament – she should be exactly the sort of dog you would like to own yourself. If at all possible, you should also try to meet her prospective husband.

If you would like a cross-bred or mongrel puppy, you are more likely to see the litter of puppies and the bitch at the same time. Try not to be too distracted by the puppies, however, as, unless they are already several weeks old, it is their mother on whom you need to concentrate at this stage.

A PURE-BRED PUPPY
Where to start

• Contact the national club of the breed in which you are interested. The club should be able to put you in touch with breeders in your area and beyond.
• Look in dog magazines or ask at your local vet centre for a contact telephone number. The staff at the centre may already know of local breeders.
• Visit local, regional and even national dog shows. You will make useful contacts there, and you will be able to chat to breeders and meet their dogs.
• If you have a friend who owns a dog of the breed that you like, and the dog is exactly the sort of animal you are after, find out where he came from. If possible, look at his pedigree and note down the names of his mother and father in case you come across them again.
• Look in the classified sections of local newspapers. Many people who own pregnant bitches but do not consider themselves professional dog-breeders will advertise litters before they are born.

What to do next

• Make a shortlist of possible breeders with suitable bitches, and then make arrangements to visit them all. Try to find out which male dogs the breeders have chosen to mate with the bitches in whom you are interested, and visit them if you can. When you go to see a bitch, do not concentrate just on the bitch herself. Take a long, hard look at her owner, too, and at the way he or she interacts with the bitch. You should get a good impression of how your puppy will be treated

TAIL-DOCKING

Laws now exist in certain countries to control the docking of puppies' tails for purely cosmetic reasons (traditionally, a boxer puppy such as this one would have had his tail docked within a few days of his birth). In the UK, the docking of puppies' tails for the sake of fashion has now been banned, but it still goes on. If, like me, you believe such procedures to be unnecessary, cruel and indefensible, make sure that the breeders on your shortlist agree with us.

in his early weeks. You should also expect to be cross-examined yourself by a good breeder as to the sort of home that you will provide for your puppy.
• Some breeds of dog suffer from serious conditions, such as hip abnormalities, that are known to be passed on from generation to generation. For some of these serious conditions, tests can be carried out on breeding animals to help in identifying those dogs and bitches most likely to pass on the problem to their puppies. Before visiting any bitch, ask your vet whether there are any special questions that you should ask the bitch's owner about both her and the male dog.

Other options

• It may seem more convenient to obtain your puppy from a friend than to carry out a proper search, but do not agree to do so simply because it is an easy option. Compromise on looks, but never on temperament.
• Dog-rescue centres have litters of pure-bred puppies who are available for re-homing from time to time. If you would like a 'rescued' puppy, keep in touch with the centres in your area. However, be very cautious about puppies who are not with their mother, as it may be difficult to predict their temperaments as adults.

A CROSS-BRED PUPPY
Where to start

• Look in local newspapers for advertisements for any litters that are about to be born, or for puppies who are already available. Ideally, they should not be more than eight weeks old (see page 68).
• Contact dog-rescue organizations in your area. They may be looking after, or may know of, a pregnant bitch or one who has whelped. If not, they will put you on a waiting list. They may also have orphaned puppies who need good homes, although, if you are a first-time dog-owner, you should really try to avoid a puppy who is not with his mother. Such a puppy may well be better off in the care of a more experienced owner.

What to do next

• If possible, visit several pregnant bitches to meet both them and their owners. If none of the bitches on your initial shortlist meets your expectations, do not take the best of a bad bunch. Be patient and keep looking, or begin to search further afield.
• If you meet a bitch with a litter of puppies several weeks old, and you like her, the puppies and the owner, you may have to decide on a particular puppy sooner than you had planned, but do not miss any of the important preparation stages detailed in the next few pages. (You will find more information on how to choose your puppy from a litter on pages 68–9.)

PLANNING AHEAD

With the research done, you should have identified the place from which you will obtain your new puppy. He may already be alive and kicking, or his egg may not even have been fertilized yet! If your puppy has been conceived but not yet born, keep in touch with the bitch's owner. Hopefully everything will go according to plan but it could be, for instance, that only five puppies are born and you are sixth on the list. If this does happen, you can either wait until the bitch is bred from again, or you must go back to the research.

If all goes well, once you know that the litter has been born, that all the puppies are healthy and that there are enough for all interested parties, you can

Planning for the adoption of a puppy is a project that will benefit from the input of all the family. The process is a particularly educational one for children.

make arrangements with the breeder to visit them to begin the selection process (see pages 68–9). You will also be able to put the date when your puppy will be seven to eight weeks old in your diary, as this is when you should collect him. You will need all the time in the interim to get ready for his arrival (see pages 50–3).

If the litter is already several weeks old by the time you first meet the puppies and their mother, you will have to get your skates on!

AN OLDER PUPPY

With an older puppy, you will need to carry out the same research (if this is possible) as for a pure-bred or cross-bred six- to eight-week-old puppy.

WARNING

Never even think about obtaining a puppy from a pet shop or market selling a wide range of breeds. Often the poor puppies sold from such places have begun their lives on 'puppy farms', where dogs are bred in totally unsuitable circumstances. Such puppies may suffer from both physical and behavioural problems.

Preparing your house and garden

As soon as you have a firm date for collecting your puppy, you can begin to prepare your house and garden for his arrival. At the very least, you will need to select a place for his bed, a playroom and a spot that he can use as his toilet. Like all puppies, he will be very inquisitive, remarkably cunning and extremely ingenious when it comes to exploring his new territory. He will test the world around him with his mouth and his teeth, in exactly the same way that babies use their hands and mouths to feel the weight and texture of all kinds of everyday substances.

IN THE GARDEN
Your garden will be full of possible hazards, and will require some preparation before your puppy arrives.

A toileting area
Right from the start, you should train your puppy to go to the toilet in a specially selected spot in your garden (see pages 74–7). As it will be much easier to clear up after him if he relieves himself on a hard surface such as concrete, you may want to prepare a suitable location. However, many puppies prefer to go to the toilet on a softer surface such as grass.

Whatever the surface, the selected spot should be away from any areas of the garden that are regularly used by you and your family, but close enough to your house so that you do not have far to go when you are toilet-training your puppy. It is also useful to have an outside tap nearby for cleaning the area.

If you have a sandpit for children, cover it over to stop your puppy from using it as an alternative toilet.

Garden security
If you intend to offer your puppy freedom in your garden, you must fence the garden to make it escape-proof. Your puppy will discover the smallest gap and, once through, he may not be able to find his way back.

Mesh-type fencing is a relatively cheap and effective option. If you can, bury this into the ground to prevent the puppy from burrowing his way out to play with the guinea-pigs next door! Fit bolts to any gates, as dogs are perfectly capable of using latches.

Potential hazards
If you have a pond, make sure that it has an escape ramp. While your puppy is very young, it will be a good idea to cover over the pond with plastic mesh,

but do not leave any gaps for your puppy to crawl through. If he does, he will still end up in the pond, but the mesh may stop him from climbing out.

Be aware of any poisonous plants in your garden, but do not dig them all up. Most dogs will have access to poisonous plants at some point in their lives, but, fortunately, they seem to avoid eating them and cases of plant poisoning are very rare. If your puppy is the exception and is fascinated by plants in your garden, you may need to fence them off or remove them.

Make sure that the door on a garden shed, and doors on any other outdoor buildings, shut properly and are lockable. Again, use your common sense.

Once your puppy arrives, you must remember to keep all garden implements locked away when you are not using them, to shut gates and doors behind you, and to take great care when using any pesticides or other chemicals in the garden. Keep your puppy away from the lawnmower, as it may throw up stones and other debris that could injure him, and, when bedding in new plants, avoid leaving name tags in the ground or old plastic plant pots lying around. Your puppy is likely to find them, destroy them and attempt to swallow the evidence.

IN THE HOUSE
You should make your home as safe as possible for your puppy, but within reason: concentrate on those places in which he is likely to be left unattended. Permanent fixtures and fittings are not the only hazards that your puppy will face. Some of the most serious dangers will be the temporary ones such as rubbish, sewing needles or cleaning chemicals that you may accidentally leave lying around. Remember that no amount of advance preparation will entirely compensate for lack of proper supervision.

A safety checklist for your garden (opposite): **1** *Install a tall perimeter fence.* **2** *Beware of any poisonous plants.* **3** *Cover a water butt.* **4** *Store tools in a shed.* **5** *Choose a toileting area with a hard surface.* **6** *Fit a hosepipe to wash the toileting area and to bath your puppy in warm weather.* **7** *Cover a pond with mesh.* **8** *Fit a dustbin with a secure lid.*

In your puppy's playroom (see page 52): **9** *Store cleaning items safely.* **10** *Vinyl flooring is easy to clean.* **11** *A puppy crate will ease toilet-training (see page 75).* **12** *Toys must be strong and safe (see page 93).* **13** *Choose a suitable food bowl (see page 65).* **14** *Refill your puppy's water bowl regularly.*

Your puppy's playroom

Think about where you are going to put your puppy's bed, or his crate if you decide to use one (see right). My recommendation would be a utility room if you have one. A vinyl or easy-clean floor is a must.

The room that you choose should be one in which you will be happy to let your puppy play, and where you can easily keep an eye on him. For the sake of hygiene and safety, it really ought to be somewhere other than the kitchen.

Spend time making sure that the room is as paw-proof and gnaw-proof as possible. Put all electric flexes out of harm's way, remove any plants and fit guards to open fireplaces. Arrange furniture to prevent your puppy from lying directly against hot radiators. Any low cupboards should have firm catches. Do not leave any of your favourite items in the room – assume that your puppy will destroy them all!

The list goes on, but I do not want it to sound like a lecture. Assume that a puppy will get into trouble if he can, and use your common sense. One final word of warning: never leave anything dangling within reach, such as a towel or a coat. I once did that and lost a whole sleeve and the entire hem from my best jacket.

House rules

What about the rest of the house? You must decide on the parts of the house to which your puppy will be allowed supervised access. This is entirely up to you (we have a rule at home, for example, that none of the animals is allowed upstairs). Remove any obvious hazards from other rooms in which your puppy will spend time, but do not leave yourself an empty cell.

Your puppy will need to learn what he can and cannot chew, and if you keep him away from everyday objects you will never be able to teach him. If while you are watching television he begins to gnaw the leg of the sofa, say 'NO' in a stern voice to break his concentration, then immediately divert his attention to something else, such as a toy (see page 93).

WHAT YOU WILL NEED

There are a number of essential dog-care items that you will require in order to look after your puppy properly. Use the information given here to compile a shopping list. By referring to other relevant sections in the book, you should be able to decide on the important features that you need to look for when purchasing each of the items on your list. Spend as much as you can afford, but make sure that you use

WHY USE A PUPPY CRATE?

A proper puppy crate will provide your puppy with a cosy den, and will also give you somewhere safe to leave him during the night and for short periods during the day when you are not able to supervise him (see below and opposite, below).

Using a crate will also make toilet-training your puppy very much easier (see page 75).

your money wisely, and avoid the temptation to buy any of the many novelties on offer. For now, it is best just to concentrate on the essentials. You may be able to borrow or hire some of the larger, more expensive items, such as a puppy crate (see page 89).

A puppy crate

A puppy crate is a metal cage with a solid metal floor and a door. Such crates are available in various sizes. Provided that you are sensible about the amount of time that your puppy spends in it, he will grow up to think of his crate as a safe den.

Even if you decide to abandon the crate when your puppy grows older and is house-trained, you may wish to use it again on a temporary basis when you go on holiday, or if your dog is ill. It is therefore worth buying a crate that is collapsible and portable, and will be big enough to accommodate your puppy when he is fully grown. He should be able to stand up in it, turn around easily and lie down fully stretched out. If you are taking on a cross-bred or mongrel puppy this may be difficult to estimate, so err on the large side.

Bedding

What will your puppy sleep on? In my view, the best option is a man-made fleece rug. This will be warm, comfortable and can go in the washing machine. Other options are a 'bean-bag' bed or a solid plastic bed with a soft cushion inside. You should avoid a traditional-style wicker basket, as this will be impossible to clean thoroughly and will be easy for your puppy to destroy.

Food and feeding equipment

You should decide what you are going to feed your puppy – and how you are going to feed it – well in advance of collecting him (see pages 54–67). Obtain the food near the time at which you need it. Buy separate feeding utensils for your puppy, including spoons or scoops to dish up his food. He will need a suitable feeding bowl and a water bowl (see page 65).

Handling equipment

Your puppy will need a collar and a lead. An extra, extending lead will also be useful for training sessions (see pages 80–7). A suitable carrying basket will make it easier for you to carry your puppy from place to place when he is very young. In a saloon car, a larger puppy should be restrained with a proper harness. If you have an estate car or hatchback, your puppy will be safer in the back behind a dog-guard, or – better still – inside a built-in car cage (see page 89).

Identity disk

Depending on any laws in force where you live, you may have to attach a disk or tag to your puppy's collar to identify him (see page 101). Even if not required by law, this may be vital in tracing him if he is lost.

Toys

Puppies have active minds as well as bodies, and, as much as your puppy's body will need exercise, so his mind will need stimulation. There are some excellent toys available, and you will only need one or two good ones at first (see page 93).

Healthcare equipment

You may already own some bathroom weighing scales; if not, you will need a set. To care for your puppy's coat, you will need some specific tools and a suitable shampoo. Keep all your old towels for him. You will need to buy parasite-prevention preparations (see pages 116–19) and dental-care items (see page 115). A first-aid kit will only be of any value if you know how to use it properly.

Hygiene equipment

You will need some special chemicals to clean up any toileting accidents indoors, and a good veterinary disinfectant. In addition, do not forget a good supply of 'pooper-scoopers'. There is a whole range available, and they are hygienic and simple to use. Test-drive a few until you find the type that you prefer!

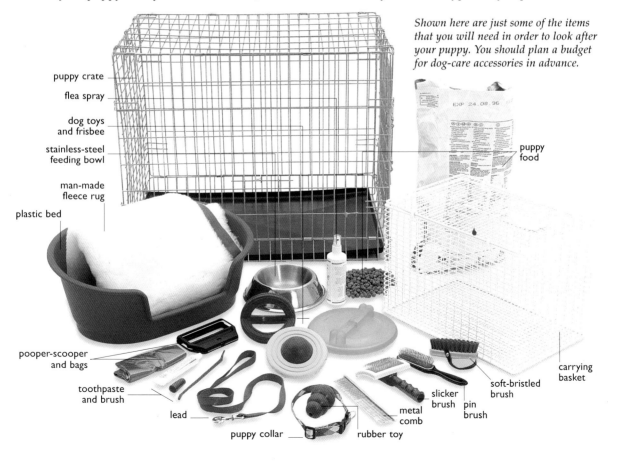

Shown here are just some of the items that you will need in order to look after your puppy. You should plan a budget for dog-care accessories in advance.

puppy crate

flea spray

dog toys and frisbee

stainless-steel feeding bowl

man-made fleece rug

plastic bed

pooper-scooper and bags

toothpaste and brush

lead

puppy collar

rubber toy

metal comb

slicker brush

pin brush

soft-bristled brush

carrying basket

puppy food

Food and drink

When it comes to dietary requirements, a puppy is a very special sort of dog. Whatever you decide to feed him, that food will have to provide his body with all the fuel that he needs to stay alive, and must contain all the essential chemicals needed for his body processes to function properly. In addition, it must supply the 'building blocks' that will allow his body to repair itself and, of course, to grow.

Good nutrition

Preparing healthy diets for dogs is a complex science, and I believe that it is best left to the skilled scientists employed by major pet-food manufacturers. However, making sure that your puppy benefits fully from their expertise by choosing the right products to feed him, and then feeding them appropriately, is up to you.

Over the next pages, you will find background information about food and digestion, with detailed advice on prepared-food options and suggestions on how to create a healthy diet for your puppy.

Feeding choices

There are so many feeding options available today that making the right decisions can seem a daunting task. However, with careful planning in advance, you will be able to devise a diet for your puppy that will fulfil all his nutritional needs.

Without a hungry puppy pestering you for his dinner, you will also be more likely to make rational choices rather than impulsive ones, so now is the best time to make the feeding decisions that will form the basis of your puppy's future diet regime. Then, all you will have to do when he is living with you is to adapt it to his personal needs as necessary (see page 65).

Asking for advice

If you are ever in doubt about nutrition, ask. There are many experts, including vets and veterinary nurses, who will help you to make the right feeding choices. Many dog-owners worry endlessly about the decisions that they have made, but you can always change your mind.

A word of warning: as soon as dog-owning friends know that you are taking on a new puppy, they may all offer you advice on feeding him. It is amazing how many self-appointed dog-nutrition experts there are! However, some may be less well-informed than they think, and speaking to too many people will also leave you very confused. Try to obtain advice only from those people who really do know about nutrition.

Your puppy will be what he eats: his meals will be transformed into everything from blood cells, nerves and muscles to skin, hair, bones and teeth. A dog is adapted to eat a wide variety of foods, but these must be balanced in order to satisfy his complex nutritional requirements. Shown here are some of the basic ingredients used to make commercially prepared dog foods (see pages 58–62).

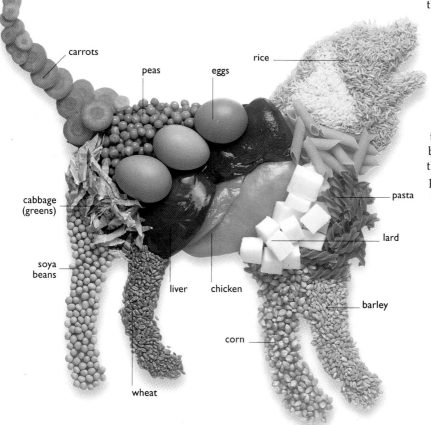

carrots · peas · eggs · rice · pasta · lard · cabbage (greens) · soya beans · liver · chicken · barley · corn · wheat

In the wild, wolves' diets will depend on where they live and the time of year. In North America in the winter, for instance, they may eat large animals such as caribou and deer; in the summer, they may add the odd hare or beaver to the menu, and may supplement their diets with berries or some grass.

WHAT IS FOOD?

My dictionary defines food as: 'that which, being digested, nourishes the body', but perhaps a better description is that food is any solid or liquid that, when swallowed, supplies any or all of the following.
• Fuel materials that the body can use to produce movement or heat.
• Materials for growth, repair or reproduction.
• Substances necessary to control the above processes.

Types of nutrient

Olive oil, meat and vegetables are all familiar food items. So are Indian take-aways, but these are more complex meals, made by mixing together different food items. What all individual foods and meals have in common is that they are made up of combinations of water and one or more of the following nutrients.

Carbohydrates • These provide energy, and can be converted into body fat. They also affect the way in which the digestive system works (see page 56).

Fats • Fats are the most concentrated source of fuel for the body. They help in the absorption of certain vitamins, and provide the essential fatty acids required for some important body functions. Fats also improve food palatability.

Proteins • When broken down, proteins provide the body with amino acids. These are the body's 'building blocks', vital for growth and repair. Proteins are used by the body to make hormones, and can also be turned into fuel, or energy.

Minerals • Present in foods in very small amounts, minerals are involved in many body functions, such as the way in which nerves work. Calcium and phosphorus are the main components of structures such as teeth and bones; other important minerals include magnesium and sodium.

Vitamins • Like minerals, vitamins are also present in foods in small quantities. They help to control many of the important chemical reactions and processes that take place in the body.

How does a dog process food?

The dog's body contains a quite remarkable food processor – his digestive system – in which food goes through a number of different stages.

The mouth • The food is first mixed with saliva to lubricate it. A dog's teeth are well-suited to breaking up chunks of food, although many dogs tend to bolt their food without chewing it.

The oesophagus • The swallowed food moves down this tube, which connects the mouth and stomach.

The stomach • Each meal, pulled to pieces when eaten, is mixed and churned up in the stomach with digestive juices, which start the breakdown and processing of proteins. The stomach also controls a steady flow of food into the intestines.

The small intestine • It is here that most digestion takes place. Fluids containing digestive enzymes are produced by the small intestine and by the pancreas (a small organ best-known for making insulin to control the body's sugar levels). Bile from the gall bladder is also added (this helps in the digestion of fats). The enzymes complete the breakdown of nutrients into units small enough to pass through the intestinal wall and into the body.

The large intestine • By the time the meal reaches the large intestine, there is little of value left in it. Bacteria digest some remaining protein and fibre.

The rectum • Any undigested materials – together with some water, minerals and dead bacteria – are stored here until the dog next goes to the toilet.

As soon as a puppy starts to eat a meal, his digestive system will begin the complex process of breaking down the food into its component parts.

The digestive system of the dog

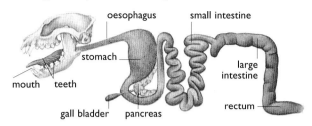

The digestive system is under nervous and hormonal control. It consists of a number of interconnected parts that all have a specific function to perform.

CREATING A HEALTHY DIET

The first step in feeding any dog a healthy diet is to work out the precise nutrients that he needs in order to prevent his body from running out of fuel, body-building materials or other essential substances. This overall requirement is called his 'nutritional need' and will depend on a number of factors, including the dog's age and lifestyle.

Thanks to years of scientific research, information is now available that specifies the known minimum nutritional need of different types of dog, including that of typical adult dogs and growing puppies. This information is very complex and of little practical use to most dog-owners. However, it is extremely valuable to the people responsible for formulating the prepared dog foods that I would recommend you to use as the basis of your puppy's diet (see pages 58–62).

Eating in the wild

Of course, there is no nutrient information to help wild dogs in choosing a diet that will keep them fit and strong. Like other animals, they become hungry because of their short-term needs for energy, or fuel – a commodity measured in calories. When hunting or foraging, their prime concern is to fill up with fuel, but they will only stay healthy in the longer term if their food not only provides enough calories, but also contains all the essential nutrients that their bodies require. Whether or not they eat far more of some nutrients than they need – a situation that in pet dogs we attempt to avoid because of concerns that some nutrients in excess may jeopardize long-term health – is less relevant to a wild animal with a short lifespan.

Your puppy will not have the opportunity to hunt and forage for his own food. His diet will be chosen by you, and your responsibility will be to ensure that you satisfy his nutritional need. So what are your options?

A totally natural diet

If you believe that your puppy should have a natural diet, you could go out to hunt and forage for him, and then simply throw a few freshly killed caribou, one or two beavers and some fruit on the kitchen floor and let him get on with it. And don't forget that you will have to show him what to do with it.

Advantage • A very natural diet.

Disadvantages • Very messy; difficult to find the right 'ingredients'; time-consuming to prepare!

Fresh human foods

You could choose to feed your puppy entirely on home-prepared fresh foods and other food items that are intended for human consumption. However, if you decide to do this, which fruits, vegetables, cereals and meats will you buy?

You will only be able to make the correct decisions about a diet of this kind for your puppy if you know precisely what nutrients each of the fresh foods contains. The ability to formulate a well-balanced diet entirely from such foods relies on a sound knowledge of the science of nutrition, as well as access to some complicated data. If you really do wish to take this option, you will therefore need expert help.

Although – with time and effort – it is certainly possible to feed a puppy properly in this way, I would not recommend you to do so.

Advantages • High-quality ingredients; can make a very palatable diet.

Disadvantages • Expensive; time-consuming to prepare; waste of fresh foods intended for human consumption; difficult to ensure a good overall nutritional balance.

Commercially prepared dog foods

You could choose to feed your puppy entirely on commercially prepared dog foods (see pages 58–62). There is now, a vast range of products from which to choose, varying greatly in both price and quality.

Advantages • Convenient; palatable; cost-effective; the best products are nutritionally well-balanced.

Disadvantages • Difficult to identify the good products from other, less good ones; reliance on manufacturers' understanding of dog nutrition; less owner-involvement.

Prepared and fresh foods

In my view, this is the best option for feeding a dog. By carefully selecting and using the very best, and most appropriate, scientifically formulated dog foods as the major part of what you feed your puppy, you will give him all the benefits that they offer.

Although it should be unnecessary, supplementing these foods with very small amounts of a range of other foods (see page 66) will help to compensate for any minor nutritional errors in the formulation, production, storage or use of the products. My own labrador retriever is fed on a complete dry food, but I let her have very small amounts of other foods as well and she always licks out my empty yoghurt pots!

Advantages • Convenient, yet allows greater owner-involvement in feeding; peace of mind for owner; palatable; cost-effective; nutritionally sound.

Disadvantages • In my opinion, none.

A puppy's digestive system is a very efficient food processor, but its powers of digestion are limited. In general, the poorer the quality of his food, the more waste he will produce.

The manufacture of commercially prepared dog foods is now a major industry. The very best companies use high-quality ingredients and advanced manufacturing processes.

COMMERCIALLY PREPARED DOG FOODS

What do dog biscuits and lightning conductors have in common? The answer is a man called James Spratt. At the end of the 19th century, Mr Spratt travelled from Ohio to London on a business trip for the purpose of selling lightning conductors. When he arrived at the quayside, however, he saw dogs eating discarded ships' biscuits, whereupon he quickly turned his attention away from lightning conductors and began to make biscuits specifically for dogs.

From those early days, the manufacture of prepared dog foods has come a very long way indeed. There are now hundreds of different products available, some of which are nutritionally much more advanced than others. So how should you choose the right products for your puppy? The best way to start, as with most things, is with the basics.

Commercially prepared dog foods are food items intended for canine consumption that have been formulated and processed by a commercial company. From now on, I will refer to them simply as prepared dog foods. From a nutritional point of view, there are only two types of prepared dog foods available.

Complete foods

All complete dog foods should contain at least the minimum recommended amounts of each nutrient required by the type of dog for whom the products are intended. However, they may contain more of certain nutrients than is known to be required. Made from many ingredients, complete foods are designed to be used as all-in-one diets without the need for any supplementation with other foods, although minor additions of certain food items should not affect the nutritional balance of the diet (see page 57). Some complete foods are sold as suitable for dogs of all ages and lifestyles, while others satisfy more specific needs, such as those of growing puppies.

Advantages • Convenient; major nutritional decisions are made by manufacturer; such foods should be easy to use (but see pages 60–1).

Disadvantages • Reliance on nutritional knowledge of manufacturers – an important consideration, as a particular product could be the sole food eaten by a dog for his entire life from weaning. In this case, even minor errors in the nutritional balance of the food could be significant in the long term.

Complementary foods

Complementary foods are intended to be fed not as a dog's entire diet, but only as a part of it. They may be made from just one ingredient or a from a number of mixed ingredients. Examples are dog treats (see page 66), 'mixer' biscuits and some 'gourmet-style' foods.

Advantage • Greater owner-involvement in feeding.

Disadvantages • Reliance on owner to make decisions as to which foods to mix and in what quantities to create a well-balanced diet; easy to overfeed.

FORMS OF PREPARED DOG FOOD

Complete and complementary dog foods may be sold in any of three forms – dry, semi-moist and moist – depending on the amount of water that they contain. These different forms of food each have a number of potential advantages and disadvantages that are worth considering in some detail.

Dry foods

Most dry foods contain between 5 and 12 per cent water. Examples include biscuits, flakes and nuggets (some dog-food products contain mixtures of these).

So-called 'mixer' biscuits are complementary dry foods that have cereals as their main ingredient, and are a peculiarly British development.

Complete dry foods, in the form of flakes, are made from a variety of plant and animal ingredients (these must be dry, so fresh animal tissues cannot be used).

Complete dry-food nuggets are made by steaming the ingredients at very high temperatures, then cutting up the cooked mixture. The individual pieces, whether stars, cubes, doughnuts or any other shapes, are dried and finally sprayed with fat.

Advantages • Good value as can be bought in bulk, and because relatively small amounts – compared with foods containing more water – need to be fed to provide the same nutritional benefit (the cost of feeding a complete dry food may be as little as one-third of that of a nutritionally equivalent moist food); left out in the air, dry foods do not spoil quickly, so they can be fed on a 'self-service' basis; some products may help to control the progression of periodontal disease (see pages 114–15); very easy and clean to use; only a slight odour is generally detectable by humans at a distance; easy to store.

Disadvantages • Perceived as 'unnatural' and 'boring' by many owners (in most cases their dogs tend to disagree); generally less digestible and also less palatable than moist foods, although palatability can be improved by adding water; shorter shelf-life than other food forms.

Semi-moist foods

Most of these foods contain between 15 and 50 per cent water. Those with the lowest water content may appear similar to dry foods, whereas those containing the most water may resemble minced or cubed meat. Individual meal portions are normally sealed in foil sachets, which are packed together in a cardboard box.

These foods are made of a mixture of meats and cereals, formed into a paste that is moulded and cut into small pieces.

Advantages • Usually have only a slight odour; can be left out in the air for longer periods than moist foods without drying out.

Disadvantages • Little choice, as only relatively few products are available in this form; generally more expensive to feed than equivalent dry foods.

PET-FOOD INGREDIENTS

Up to 98 per cent of all prepared pet foods sold in the UK are made by companies belonging to the Pet Food Manufacturers' Association. As members of this association, the manufacturers agree to use only materials from animals fit for human consumption.

They also guarantee to use nothing from horses, ponies, whales, seals or kangaroos, and use only tuna caught in a way that does not endanger dolphins.

Moist foods

Most moist foods contain between 60 and 85 per cent water. Some are pressure-cooked in their containers or in a large vat; others are made simply by preparing fresh ingredients and then freezing them without pre-cooking. Typical ingredients are different meats, fish, vegetables and cereals. Some products may even contain other prepared food items, such as pasta.

Advantages • Generally more palatable than other food forms; wide choice of products available; long shelf-life (particularly in the case of canned foods).

Disadvantages • More expensive than equivalent dry foods; more messy to use; products dry out if left in the air, so should not be fed on a 'self-service' basis.

Prepared dog foods may be sold in the three forms shown below. None is necessarily nutritionally 'better' than the others; each has both advantages and disadvantages.

moist food

dry food   semi-moist food

USING PREPARED DOG FOODS

It is impossible to choose or use prepared dog foods properly without understanding the information provided on the product labels. Much useful advice is to be found here, and it will help you to select the most suitable products for your puppy and to feed them properly. There are laws that dictate what must be stated on a dog-food label and where it should be printed. Most of the important information that you need to look for is normally all in one place on the label – but rarely, if ever, is this on the front!

In the UK (this may vary from country to country depending on the national laws relating to dog-food labelling) there are currently eight important questions about a prepared dog food to which you should be able to find answers.

Who is the food intended for?

If the label just states that it is a food for dogs, then it must be suitable for dogs of all ages, from weaning to very old age. Some products are intended for specific types of dog – such as puppies or older dogs – and the best manufacturers will define what they mean by this. For example, the label may state that the food is for puppies of up to 12 months old, or for dogs of more than seven years old. Do not choose a food for your puppy that is intended for cats.

What type of food is it?

Is it a complete or a complementary food? You must find out, as this will affect the other feeding decisions that you need to make. Remember: a complete food does not need any supplementation; a complementary food does (see page 58).

What is the food made from?

You will find a list of ingredients on the label, although this may not be as informative as you might imagine. Manufacturers may list every ingredient separately, or, as is normally the case, may only list ingredients in groups, such as 'meat and animal derivatives', 'cereals' or 'derivatives of vegetable origin'. The ingredients list should be written in decreasing order by weight.

How much of each nutrient is there?

Look for what is called the typical analysis, which lists the protein, oil (fat) and ash (effectively the total amount of minerals in the food). The quantity of each will be given either as a percentage by weight, or as the amount per 100 g (4 oz) of the food. The analysis will tell you how much fibre the food contains, and

---

NOTE ON NUTRIENTS

Unless you understand your puppy's precise needs for all the different types of nutrient, do not try to choose a dog food for him based on the typical analysis on the label. In my view, this information is of no value to the vast majority of dog-owners, although it is useful to those of us who advise them.

Also, never be tempted to compare the percentages or amounts listed in the typical analysis on one label with those on another. If the two foods are in different forms – one moist and the other dry, for instance – the amounts shown may be very misleading.

---

may also indicate its water content. With regard to vitamins, depending on the law of the land, only certain vitamins need to be listed if they are added separately. The amount of carbohydrate included can be calculated from the other figures.

Does the food contain additives?

Extra vitamins, flavours, preservatives and colouring agents are all examples of additives used in certain dog foods. Additives tend to have a bad reputation, but many of them are essential in ensuring that the product is safe and nutritious to eat, and they should only be used in the smallest amounts necessary. When any preservatives or colouring agents have been used, it should say so on the label.

Is the food fresh?

A 'best-before' date should be printed or stamped somewhere on the packet (this may well be on the container itself, rather than on the label).

Who makes the food?

If you require more information about a particular food, such as the way in which the product has been tested (see page 62), you will need to contact the company responsible for the food: an address should be supplied on the label.

How should the food be used?

You will find feeding instructions on the label. If it is a complementary food, the label should tell you what else you need to feed. As every dog is an individual, it is impossible for any manufacturer to give precise and specific feeding instructions to suit all dogs for whom a product is intended. Instead, suggestions will be offered in the form of feeding guides, although, for no logical reason, these guides are often very unclear. For instance, many feeding guides on canned complete foods will tell you that you can either offer the food on its own, or with mixer biscuits, yet the two options are nutritionally different.

If you find a particular feeding guide on a product confusing, my advice would be to choose another product. On a well-labelled food, the guide should be self-explanatory. Remember, however, that the suggested amount to feed each day is only a starting point: you will need to adjust the quantity that you offer your puppy depending on his condition and his weight (see page 63). Take careful note of any special advice that is offered in the feeding guide about the preparation of the food or its use.

SELECTING A PREPARED FOOD

Ultimately, the decision as to which food product or products you use will be a very personal one. For instance, you may have had great success in the past with the products made by a particular manufacturer and wish to use their foods again.

Asking the experts

If the puppy that you are about to get will be the first dog that you have looked after, asking the advice of a person knowledgeable about nutrition will save you a lot of time and effort, and also a great deal of worry.

Every person who has ever fed a dog will offer an opinion on how to feed your puppy: listen to what they have to say, as some of the advice will be useful (especially practical hints and tips on feeding), but beware of the views of self-proclaimed 'nutrition experts'. In my experience, many such 'experts' don't even know what they don't know! One good option is to ask your vet, or a veterinary nurse who is interested in dog nutrition, what he or she would use to feed the puppy you plan to have. Alternatively, if you would like to be more involved in making the final decision, you could ask for a shortlist of several suitable products from which you can choose.

Dogs of different ages have different nutritional needs. This puppy and older dog will each benefit from foods specifically formulated to meet their individual requirements.

HOW ARE DOG FOODS TESTED?

If a food claims that it is complete, the claim must be justified. After all, the food may be a dog's sole source of nutrients throughout his life, so any minor errors in its formulation could affect his long-term health.

The very best foods will have been tested by both of the methods described here, but, unfortunately, most food labels do not state how the products have been tested.

You may therefore have to write to the manufacturer in order to obtain this information.

LABORATORY ANALYSIS
The purpose of these tests is to find out what a food contains. Provided that it has enough of the correct nutrients to match the minimum nutritional requirements of a dog for whom it is intended, the manufacturer can call the food complete. However, these tests check the quantities of nutrients in a food, not their quality. One scientist is reputed to have put old leather boots, some engine oil and some vitamin-and-mineral powder through this analysis, and it came out as suitable to be sold as a complete food! His rather unusual ingredients may have contained the appropriate amounts of the correct nutrients, but the quality of those nutrients would make them impossible for any dog to digest properly.

FEEDING TRIALS
These tests are used to measure the quality of the ingredients. The food that is under test is fed to a group of appropriate dogs, and scientists then measure how the dogs get on and how well the food is digested.

Tips on prepared foods

The feeding advice that I offer my clients is as follows.
• Aim to select just one brand of complete food. This should account for at least 90 per cent of everything that your puppy eats (see also page 66).
• Choose a food that is specifically formulated for growing puppies. Avoid any food that claims to be suitable for any dog of any age.
• Choose a food made by a reputable company, and find out how the food has been tested. Only select foods tested by both laboratory analysis and feeding trials (see above).
• With a dry food, check on the label that an animal-protein source is one of the first three ingredients listed (on a moist food, this should be one of the first two ingredients listed).
• When comparing the relative costs of different foods, do not look just at the actual prices of the products.

Instead, calculate approximately how much of each food your puppy will need to eat per day, and then estimate the daily feeding cost of each food. Remember that, as a general rule, a dog will need to eat less of a more expensive food than he would need of a cheaper one in order to stay healthy.
• Spend as much as you can afford. Cheap foods tend to contain cheap ingredients, whereas the more expensive foods will be made from better-quality ingredients and by companies that are more likely to have invested in research and product development.
• Choose products that are clearly labelled with comprehensive feeding instructions. Always follow these instructions carefully.
• Finally, remember that you can always change your mind at a later stage, if necessary. The scientific excellence of a food will be irrelevant if it remains in your puppy's bowl because he dislikes it.

FEEDING YOUR PUPPY

When you bring your puppy home, you will be able to put all this theory on feeding into practice. When you collect your puppy, make sure that you find out from his breeder exactly what he has been fed on since weaning, and ask if you can buy a small amount of that food to feed him for the first few days.

Professional breeders often tend to have very strong opinions about how to feed puppies. Some are very knowledgeable and up-to-date while others have more traditional views, but don't let either type influence the choices that you have made. Provided that you have been sensible about how you have reached your decision, and have obtained expert advice, stick by it.

First things first

On day one, feed your puppy the diet to which he is accustomed, and then, on day two, begin to mix in some of the new food that you have chosen. He may turn his nose up at this food at first. If it is a dry food, read the label and see whether you can add a little water, but do not make the food really 'mushy': just add enough water to soften it. If you are offering a moist food, warm it a little. Be patient. If all goes well, the puppy should be completely on to his new food by the end of the first week. However, if he continues to refuse the food, contact your vet centre for advice.

The amount that a puppy needs to eat will depend on the type and quality of food that he is given. Each of the bowls shown below contains a daily portion of a complete food suitable for this 12-month-old elkhound.

How much to feed?

The total amount of food that your puppy needs each day will depend not only on the food itself, but also on the puppy's weight, his activity level and the rate at which his body burns up calories even when he is asleep. Every puppy is different when it comes to energy requirements, and even two puppies of the same age, sex, weight and breed are likely to need slightly different amounts of the same food in order to stay healthy and to grow properly.

Weighing your puppy • The only sensible way to start is to weigh your puppy, and then to follow the feeding guide on the product label. This should recommend the amount of food that puppies of different weights need each day, measured either in grammes (ounces) or by the number of tins or cartons required. If your puppy's weight lies between the weight examples given in the guide, make a sensible estimate. Make sure that you measure out the food portions accurately. By regularly weighing your puppy and then comparing his weight with the feeding guide, you will be able to adjust the amount of food that you give him as he grows.

Development checks • Your vet or a veterinary nurse should keep a careful check on how your puppy is developing at his regular health-check appointments at your vet centre (see page 71). He or she should be happy to make any further feeding suggestions as appropriate, and will help you with any queries that you may have.

reasonable-quality complete
dry-food mixture

higher-quality complete
dry-food nuggets

high-quality complete
moist food

reasonable-quality complete
moist food

How many meals a day?

Young puppies have small stomachs, and need their daily food split into manageable portions to prevent their digestive systems from being overloaded. As a general guide, once he is weaned, your puppy should be fed three or four times a day until he is half his expected adult body weight. From then on, you can cut down to two meals a day.

Depending on the type of food that you give your puppy, it should be possible to get him down to one meal a day by the time he is fully grown (see page 67). Whether you end up feeding him once or twice a day is up to you, but remember that the total quantity that he eats each day must be the same. A disadvantage of twice-daily feeding is that any small errors in the amounts fed are likely to be doubled.

If you are in any doubt about adjusting the number of meals that you offer your puppy, speak to your vet or a veterinary nurse.

Who should do the feeding?

Your puppy will learn to respect the hand that feeds him, so this is really a job in which every member of the family should be involved. Feeding time is also a very good opportunity for older children to reinforce their dominance over a puppy, by running through a simple training routine with him (see pages 82–5) immediately before offering the food.

When to feed?

Try to spread your puppy's meals evenly through the day, and do not feed him just before exercising him, as he will want to sleep on a full stomach. After eating he will probably want to go to the toilet, so do not feed him just before you go to bed or go out, without giving him the chance to empty his bowels.

Remember, too, that your puppy is a pack animal and would prefer to eat with the other members of his 'pack'. If you sit down and eat three meals a day as a family, feed your puppy at the same times. However, avoid feeding him just before you eat or he may begin to believe that he has a 'special' status in your family.

Feeding time is a good opportunity to practise basic training routines. You will be sure to have your puppy's full attention, and he will see his meal as a powerful reward (see page 81). Older children should be involved in all aspects of caring for a puppy, including feeding him.

If you decide to feed your puppy a dry food, you will need an airtight container in which to store it.

Where to feed?

This is entirely up to you, but I would recommend feeding your puppy in a place away from where you eat. He should be allowed to eat in peace and quiet as, if people or other animals are about, he may feel that his food could be stolen from him if he does not eat it quickly, and may gorge himself.

On the other hand, if he is fussy about his food, the threat of competition may make him concentrate on it better. I feed my labrador retriever outdoors.

What to feed in?

You should buy your puppy's food bowl in advance. In my experience, the best bowls are made of stainless steel, and are wider at the base than they are at the top. Bowls of this type are easy to keep clean, virtually indestructible and very stable.

Go for a bowl with a non-slip base so that your puppy cannot turn it into an ice-hockey puck. It should be of suitable dimensions for a puppy of the size and type that you have chosen. A shallow, wide bowl is better than a narrow, deep one, as it will take longer for your puppy to eat a meal that is spread thinly than one that is stacked up in a heap ready for excavation in a single mouthful.

Avoid bowls that are designed to contain both food and water – the water may end up as soup.

What about variety?

Many dogs seem very happy to eat the same food every day for long periods. Assume that your puppy is going to be one of them. At first, it is much better to concentrate on feeding one high-quality complete food and feeding it properly, rather than trying to 'mix and match' a number of different foods.

If, after a time, your puppy begins to refuse a food that he has been perfectly happy to eat for some time, it may be that he is a dog who would benefit from a little variety in his diet. Some brands of food may be available in different varieties, so, provided that all these varieties are equivalent from a nutritional point of view, you should be able to solve the problem without having to search for alternative brands that are nutritionally equivalent.

Fussy eaters

Avoid selecting foods for your puppy simply because he finds them tasty, as the most palatable foods are not necessarily the best for him. Offering too much variety may also get you into problems, as your puppy may continually accept and then reject new foods in the knowledge that you are likely to provide him with something else. You will then run out of good-quality foods to offer, and – like many owners who end up in this situation – you will probably resort to highly palatable, unbalanced foods in order to keep your puppy happy. A big mistake!

CHECKING ON PROGRESS

If you are anything like many of the puppy-owners to whom I speak, you will worry yourself silly about whether you have made the right feeding choices for your puppy. Don't. The most important test of the feeding regime that you have adopted is to take a close look at your puppy and at the waste he produces, and this is one of the reasons why regular health-checks at your vet centre are so important. Ideally, once a month your puppy should go to see his veterinary nurse, who will make sure that he is growing at the correct rate. By weighing him, the nurse can create a personal growth chart to compare with normal charts for puppies of his type (see page 35), to check that he is not getting fat.

What about other foods?

As has been discussed (see page 58), complete dog foods are designed to be fed on their own. However, I would recommend that, if you wish, you should feel free to add to your puppy's diet very small amounts of other food items, such as those listed below. Provided that the food items are chosen with care, and account for 10 per cent or less of his daily food allowance, they should not adversely affect the overall balance of your puppy's diet. Items to avoid adding are the fatty foods that are high in calories.

Fresh meat • This should be cooked, not raw, and fit for you to eat. Never let your puppy chew the meat from cooked bones (see opposite).

Fish • This is a good source of protein, but is low in important minerals and vitamins. Bones should be removed to prevent choking. Always cook fish first; never feed it raw.

Eggs • If possible, feed egg yolks and whites together. If fed on their own, egg whites must be cooked: when raw, they contain a substance that can destroy an important B vitamin.

Cheese • This is a good source of protein and fat, but watch the extra calories.

Prepared dog treats • There are plenty of these to choose from, and your puppy will love them. But remember that the way to a dog's heart is not just through his stomach. In the UK around two million dogs are overweight, and most have ended up that way because – when it came to these treats – they couldn't say no and neither could their owners.

There is a whole range of dog treats available, but if you will not be able to resist your puppy's pleading looks you should make sure that your house is a snack-free zone.

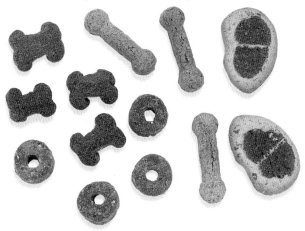

WARNING

If you decide to alter or adapt your puppy's diet, make the changes gradually by mixing some of his new and old food together. After a few days of this, you can change over completely to the new food. Any sudden alterations to his diet – even between two good-quality foods – are likely to give your puppy diarrhoea.

Liver • This is most nutritious if fed raw in small amounts, but may cause diarrhoea. Cut liver into tiny pieces and oven-bake it for a useful, highly palatable training reward (see page 81).

Vegetables • These are low in protein and fat, and high in fibre. Vegetables make very good training rewards for those who like the taste, as they are low in calories. Watch out for wind!

Table scraps • Avoid giving your puppy sauces and other human food dressings, as many of these are very rich and may upset his digestion.

What about special supplements?

You may be tempted to add some of the following to your puppy's diet, but read on and think again.

Fats and oils • These are very high in calories. A component of fat – linoleic acid – is important in maintaining good coat quality, and many owners add fats and oils to their dogs' diets in the hope of giving them glossier coats. However, dogs fed on a high-quality complete food should not need them. Fats and oils are both very concentrated sources of energy, or calories, and so even small quantities may have an adverse effect on the overall nutritional balance of your puppy's diet.

Vitamins and minerals • These are essential if a home-made diet is being fed (see page 57), but are totally unnecessary and potentially harmful if a good-quality prepared food is being used.

Chocolate • Highly palatable and highly fattening, chocolate contains a substance that is poisonous to dogs. Unsweetened baking chocolate is the most dangerous – never feed this to your puppy.

Onions and garlic • These cause bad breath. In large quantities, onions are poisonous to dogs.

Herbal and plant supplements • Few, if any, health-benefit claims have been proven scientifically. That is not to say that these supplements do not work, but be careful. Some of the most powerful drugs are plant extracts, and many herbs and other plants can be poisonous to dogs if fed in the wrong amounts.

What about bones?

Your puppy may enjoy gnawing at bones, but they will be of little or no nutritional value. And, contrary to popular opinion, chewing on bones is not likely to prevent him suffering from gum disease (see page 115). Bones can actually be very harmful: they could break your puppy's teeth and, if swallowed, fragments of bone could become lodged in his stomach or intestines.

If you insist on giving your puppy a bone, ensure that it is a large knuckle bone, and only let him have it as a special treat for a maximum of half an hour each day. Never offer your puppy small cooked bones.

Moving on to adult food

If, as I have recommended, you have chosen to feed a complete food specifically formulated for growing puppies, you should change your puppy on to a complete food for adult dogs at or near the time when he stops growing. Some puppies of the small and toy breeds may reach their adult body weights at about six months of age; others of the giant breeds may not

Water plays a vital role in keeping a dog healthy. The daily quantity of water that your puppy will require will depend on a range of factors, including his body weight. This young golden retriever is likely to need about 1.5 litres (2 pints) of water per day.

mature until they are over one year old. The feeding guide on the puppy food that you have chosen should indicate when to make this change, and is likely to recommend a product made by the same company that will be suitable from this point onwards.

WATER

A dog can survive for weeks without food, but will only remain alive for a few days at the most without water. Water enables the body's essential chemical reactions to take place. It is the main component of blood, is very involved in body-temperature control and is essential for digestion. A typical adult golden retriever's body contains about 18 litres (4 gallons) of water, accounting for 60 per cent of his body weight.

Inputs and outputs

As with all dogs, your puppy will be constantly losing water from his body in his faeces and urine, in the air that he breathes out (especially when panting), in the small amount of sweat that he produces through his feet and nose, and in other body secretions. All the water that he loses each day must be replaced. Some of what he needs will be produced by his body as it burns up food to produce energy, but most will either come as part of his food, or through drinking water.

How much water does a dog need?

An average adult golden retriever will require about 1.5 litres (2 pints) of water every day, which he will obtain from his food and from drinking. The amount that he drinks may be influenced by how much water he takes in with his food: remember that a can of moist prepared dog food may contain 85 per cent water, whereas a dry food may contain only 5 per cent. As it is impossible to know exactly how much water your puppy will need each day, you should make sure that he always has access to plenty of fresh drinking water. He can then adjust his water intake to suit himself.

WHAT ABOUT OTHER DRINKS?

Fresh, clean tap water is the only kind of drink that your puppy should need. Some owners feel that they should give their puppies milk to drink as well. Cows' milk is very nutritious, but, if your puppy is eating a good-quality, well-balanced puppy food, he will not need it. In fact, he may find it difficult to digest milk properly, and it could give him diarrhoea as a result.

Choosing your puppy

Most dog-behaviour experts agree that the best age for a puppy to be moved to his new home is when he is seven to eight weeks old. Adoption before seven weeks may affect his future relationships with other dogs, while remaining with his litter too long may affect his behaviour towards people.

Picking from a litter

When choosing a young puppy from a litter, try to visit the litter that you have selected several times, in order to gain a good impression of the characters of the individual puppies. Remember that there is no single 'best' puppy in a litter: each will have his own good and bad points.

Each time you visit, observe the whole litter from a distance before interacting with the puppies yourself. It is very tempting – particularly for children – just to dive into the middle of the litter to play with them, but try to avoid acting on impulse.

Instead, follow the steps given here, and you will be much more likely to end up with the right puppy for you and your family.

WARNING

You should be extremely cautious about agreeing to take on a puppy without knowing anything about his background – for example, if he is at a rescue centre. Seek professional guidance before making a decision, and do not take on a puppy simply because you feel sorry for him: you may not be sufficiently experienced to care for him properly. The best rescue centres now employ animal-behaviour experts to help match owners to dogs needing new homes.

1 Arrange your final visit to the litter when the puppies are seven to eight weeks old. If possible, all those who will live with your puppy and will help to look after him should go with you, but make sure that they understand what to do when you get there.

If you will be taking the puppy home the same day, make sure that you are prepared for him at home (see pages 50–3), that you have the equipment to transport him safely in the car (see page 89) and that you have made an appointment for him to be checked by your vet, if possible on the way home (see page 71).

2 At the breeder's house, spend 15 to 20 minutes watching the puppies playing and interacting with their mother. Try to form a view as to the temperament of each puppy, and ask the breeder what he or she thinks of each of them. If you are a first-time owner, it is wise to avoid the most outgoing puppy, as he may be a bit of a handful. Conversely, a timid puppy may not be a good idea if you will expect him to live in a bustling household. For most families, a puppy who is not too cocky, but not too shy and retiring, is a good choice.

On your first visit to meet a breeder or see a litter, spend time with the bitch to be bred from (or the puppies' mother). If she is not exactly the kind of dog that you would like to have, go no further.

By watching a litter of puppies playing, you will gain some idea of their individual temperaments. However, remember that the way a puppy behaves with his litter mates may change when he is separated from them (see page 32).

3 Next, look just at the puppies in whom you are interested. At first, sit on the floor and see how they interact with you. Again, confirm in your own mind which puppy is the boldest. Is the one that you thought to be timid hanging back? Then play with the puppies a little. A dominant puppy may take control of any game, and is likely to grow into a spirited adult.

Take a closer look at each puppy, and carry out a simple health-check (see pages 108–9). If you are in doubt about anything, ask the breeder.

4 Making the final choice is never easy – you will probably want to take all the puppies home! Tell the breeder your decision, and explain that this is subject to the approval of your vet. When you leave, you should have the following items.
• A receipt for the money that you have paid.
• Your puppy's pedigree-registration papers (if any).
• His vaccination record (if any).
• His worming record.
• His medical record, which should include details of any treatments carried out by his breeder or a vet.
• Feeding notes, including timings and size of meals.
• A piece of your puppy's bedding, so that he will have something that smells familiar in his new home.

Choosing an older puppy

Spend time with any older puppy in whom you are interested: play with him and take him for a walk. If you think that a particular puppy is wonderful and will suit you well but you would like a second opinion, it would be a good idea to ask a veterinary nurse or animal-behaviour expert to come along and have a look at the puppy with you.

Carry out a simple health-check on your favourite puppy before making a final decision (see pages 108–9). This will enable you to pick up any obvious health problems, and to see how tolerant he is of being handled (see page 70).

Your puppy at home

With all the important preparations made well in advance, the real fun can begin. However, there is still work to do: you must settle your puppy into his new home, and toilet-training should get underway from the start. Now is the time to put all the theory into practice, to give your puppy the fulfilling life he deserves.

Collecting your puppy

If you have chosen a young puppy from a litter, you should collect him when he is seven to eight weeks old (see page 68). Even if you have decided on an older puppy (see page 69), you should still be ready at home for his arrival before you collect him. Your vet and veterinary nurse should be expecting to see you later on. It is going to be an exciting and potentially stressful day for all of you. Do not expect miracles,

You should take your puppy home in a proper carrying basket. The strongest type is made of plastic-coated wire, but a flat-packed plastic or tough cardboard carrier will do.

as your puppy may be a little over-awed by so many new experiences. If you are well-prepared, however, you should take it all in your stride.

Lifting a puppy

There are two ways to do this properly. Children and people with small hands normally find it easiest to scoop up a puppy with one arm under his chest and the other behind his bottom. He will then sit on their arms. If you have large hands, pick up the puppy by grasping either side of his chest, almost in the same way that you might pick up a baby. As you bring him close to your body, you can move your arms into the position that someone smaller would use.

Hold the puppy firmly, but do not 'bear-hug' him. If you hold him very tightly he is likely to wriggle, but carried firmly and close to your body he will feel safe and secure. Avoid carrying him under one arm. When you put your puppy down, place him on the ground: do not let him jump out of your arms.

TRAVELLING HOME

Ideally, you should take someone else with you when you collect your puppy, so that one of you can look after him while the other concentrates on driving.

Most young puppies who are no bigger than adult cats will travel well in a pet's carrying basket, with a piece of man-made fleece rug (see pages 52–3) for bedding. Your puppy may go to the toilet on the way home, so place some newspaper under the bedding.

Where to put your puppy

If you are travelling by car, your puppy's basket must be secure. Placing it in a footwell should ensure that he is well-protected in case you should have to brake suddenly. In addition, you will avert possible damage to your car upholstery if he goes to the toilet. An alternative is to secure the basket on the back seat, using one of the rear seatbelts, and to protect the upholstery with a plastic sheet or an old towel. If you have an estate car, you could put the basket in the back, but make sure that it cannot slide about. Do not put your puppy in the boot of a saloon car.

Restraining a large puppy

A puppy who is too big to fit in a normal carrying basket should be restrained in a proper harness that attaches to a conventional seatbelt. He will also be safe behind a dog-guard or, better still, in a proper car cage (see page 89), but do not give him too much space or he will slide about. Fill up most of the back of an estate car with cardboard boxes so that his movement is restricted.

This may be your puppy's first trip in a car, so take it steadily and avoid Grand-Prix-style accelerating or sudden braking. The puppy may suffer from motion sickness, and driving like this will make him worse.

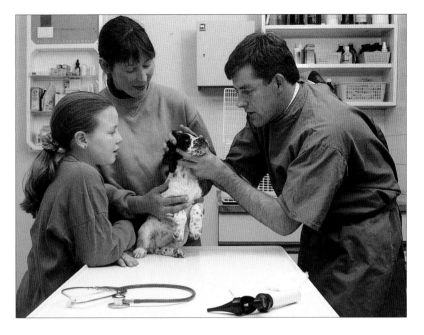

Your vet will examine your puppy very thoroughly to make sure that he is fit and well, and is not suffering from any developmental disorders.

AT YOUR VET CENTRE

If your puppy is unvaccinated (see page 121), keep him in the car until your appointment. You will not know what animals have been in the waiting room on that day, or what they were suffering from, and although the risks are slight it is best to be cautious.

What will your vet do?

Your vet will give your puppy a thorough check-over to make sure that he is fit and well and is not suffering from any obvious developmental problems. If there does turn out to be something wrong, he or she will help you to decide what action to take.

The vet or a veterinary nurse should weigh your puppy and enter his weight on a new medical record. They will also ask to see the papers that you obtained from his breeder, to check on any previous medical treatments and to see how he has been wormed.

Depending on your puppy's exact age and on the policy of your vet centre, your vet may suggest giving him a vaccine while you are there (see page 121). The veterinary nurse may even administer a worming dose (see pages 116–18). If you have decided to have your puppy permanently identified with a microchip (see page 101), this may also be organized then and there.

Final queries

Now is the time to clarify any issues about which you are uncertain: your vet or nurse should be happy to run through with you again any matters that you may have discussed when planning for your puppy's arrival home. Make sure that, before you leave, you know exactly when and how to worm your puppy, when he needs vaccinations and when you should bring him back to the centre for his next development check. Finally, pay the bill and take your puppy home.

FITTING YOUR PUPPY'S COLLAR

Place the collar around your puppy's neck, and fasten it so that you can slip two fingers on edge beneath it without pulling the collar tight. He will find wearing a collar around his neck a strange sensation at first, so although he is unlikely to try to remove it he will almost certainly scratch at it. However, with so much else going on in his life, the collar should not trouble him for long.

Welcome home

Try to structure your puppy's first day at home with you, rather than making up what you do with him as you go along. Stick to the mealtimes to which he is accustomed, and be prepared to start toilet-training him straight away (see pages 74–7).

Your puppy will enjoy exploring his surroundings and it will be tempting to play with him all day, but remember to let him rest. You will need to introduce him to everyone who shares his home, but do not invite all your friends around immediately.

This is a great day for your family and your puppy. It is the start of a new way of life for you all. Enjoy it!

SUPERVISING YOUR PUPPY

At first, you must keep an eye on your puppy at all times. You may be convinced that your house and garden are puppy-proof (see pages 50–2), but he will be better qualified to put your preparations to the test.

If, as I recommend, you have decided to use a puppy crate (see page 52), you should start to accustom your puppy to it straight away. Put him in it when he has eaten and is sleepy.

Toileting

As soon as you arrive home, take your puppy to his toileting area, as it may have been some time since he last relieved himself. Do not expect him to go straight away, however, as he will almost certainly want to have a little look around. Wait with him. This will be his very first toilet-training lesson, so use the correct command (see pages 74–5) – even though he may not even recognize your voice or his name yet – and praise him when he has finished. Then take him indoors.

Feeding your puppy

Your puppy may have only just arrived home, but he may already be hungry and tired. If not, you can get on and start all the necessary introductions (see opposite), but remember that you want him to be tired, but not exhausted, when you first put him in his bed or puppy crate to sleep. Trying to time his first sleep so that it coincides with his first meal is a good idea, as eating the meal should help him to drop off.

If it is time for a meal, and especially if the puppy is showing signs of tiredness, prepare his food and offer it to him near his crate or in his feeding area. Casually observe him feeding, but do not stand over him.

Putting your puppy to bed

When he has finished eating, take your puppy outside again in case he wants to go to the toilet, and then settle him into his bed or crate to sleep. Placing the piece of bedding that you have brought back from his old home will make his new den smell like the one he has just left. A covered hot-water bottle under the bedding will also give him some extra warmth.

Without too much fuss, quietly close the door and leave him in peace. Expect the puppy to start whining – this is probably the first time that he has slept alone – but do not run back in to comfort him straight away. Remember that whining is his way of telling his family where he is. You already know that, so bite your lip and leave him. He must start learning from day one that, when he is alone, you will come back without his having to call you (see also pages 94–5).

If your puppy continues to whine, he may simply not be sufficiently tired. Given enough time, he will certainly fall asleep, but you may give in before that happens. If you do go back to him, do not cuddle and praise him: just open the crate door, let him wander out and start the introductions (see below). When he can no longer keep his eyes open, put him back to bed.

If possible, try not to let your puppy wake up alone, or he will probably start whining again. You will have to go to him when he wakes because he will want to go to the toilet and play, and, if he is already whining when you go to him, he is likely to believe that you have turned up because he called you. Next time he is on his own, he may therefore whine again rather than waiting to see if you appear without being summoned. If you have a baby-listening device, use it.

FAMILY INTRODUCTIONS

Getting to know his new family will be your puppy's biggest priority. You may be tempted constantly to pick him up and cuddle him, but you should give him the opportunity to investigate you in his own time.

Children

If you have children, make sure that they stay calm. Let them stroke the puppy when he comes near, but the less squealing and laughing the better.

Your puppy may already be very confident, and even the slightest encouragement will make him over-excited. In this case, stroke him and talk to him. He will almost definitely 'mouth' you, and his needle-sharp teeth may come as quite a shock, especially to children. Make an appropriate noise to let your puppy know that this hurts, and then divert his attention to something else, such as a toy. Do the same if he tries to pull and play with your clothing or the furniture.

Other dogs

Introductions to any other dogs will depend on their temperaments. A young dog who is used to others is likely to accept a young puppy with no problem; an older dog may need to be introduced more gradually. Whatever his temperament, put an existing dog on a lead so that you have good control over him when you first make the introduction. A bouncing, over-excited first encounter may be as alarming to your puppy as an unfriendly greeting. Supervise any introductions until you are happy that the older dog will not harm your puppy, and that your puppy will not pester him.

Cats

Most cats will be naturally afraid of a strange puppy, and their instinct will be to run and hide. Some very territorial cats may stand their ground and even attack. If you have a cat, restrain your puppy when the cat is nearby, as any sudden movements from the puppy

HANDLING YOUR PUPPY

Can you imagine how a puppy must feel when a person suddenly grabs him from behind? Whenever you are interacting with your puppy, it is very important that he knows where you are and what is happening.

First of all, get down to his level so that you will be less intimidating to him. Make sure that you have your puppy's attention before handling him in any way, and talk to him about what you are doing. Keeping up constant one-way conversations like this is the best way of accustoming your puppy to the sound of your voice.

may scare him. Reward your puppy for staying calm (see page 81). When both your cat and puppy are in the house but you cannot supervise them, keep them separated. Over time they should become friends, and may even come to share the same bed.

OBEYING THE RULES

Allow your puppy to explore your house and garden with you, but – right from the start – enforce the basic house rules that you devised when preparing for his arrival (see page 52). Be prepared to add new rules as and when they become necessary.

Try not to be too 'soft', just because your puppy is small and cute. Allowing him to cuddle up to you at night on your bed may seem appealing, particularly if he begins to whine when you leave him on his own, but you should beware of making this an acceptable rule. Will you still want him snoring into your ear when he is an adult? Right from the start, he should learn to cope when he is alone (see pages 94–5).

Toilet-training

Pet dogs are naturally clean animals in their toileting habits, and even from a very young age puppies instinctively leave their nests to empty their bowels and to urinate. In the wild, this instinctive behaviour helps to prevent disease, particularly that caused by parasites such as intestinal worms (see pages 116–18).

Toileting behaviour

The fact that your puppy is 'pre-programmed' in this way is what makes it possible to toilet-train him at all, but you will need to be patient. Knowing the basics about natural dog-toileting behaviour will help you to understand the principles of toilet-training, so that you can develop a method to suit you and your puppy.

Your puppy's digestive system constantly produces waste. Drip after drip, his two kidneys are dribbling urine down into his bladder 24 hours a day. Several times a day, the puppy's nervous system sends signals to his brain that start a pattern of instinctive behaviour that will lead to the removal of the accumulated waste from his body. The cause of this nervous activity may be that another meal is entering his system, or that his rectum or bladder is physically full.

Finding a good spot

Whatever the cause, your puppy's behaviour will be much the same. He will try to find a suitable place to go to the toilet, he will adopt the necessary body position, and he will go. But what will he consider an appropriate place? At around three weeks old, his only aim would have been to go away from his nest. As he became older and more mobile, he will probably have wandered further afield, but probably not outdoors.

Subconsciously, the sights and smells of the places in which his breeder allowed him to go to the toilet will have become fixed in your puppy's brain, so when he arrives home with you he will choose a place that looks and smells similar.

For instance, his breeder may have covered the floor around his nest with newspaper. The nest area may have been near the kitchen, and so shared some of its smells. When your puppy arrives at your house, the only newspapers may be in a pile on the coffee table in your living-room, next door to your kitchen, so somewhere between the two may seem a perfectly acceptable toileting spot.

This is a simplistic view of a complex process that occurs inside a puppy's body when he needs to go to

TOILETING TIPS

• Whenever your puppy goes to the toilet, ensure that he is in the same place – his designated toileting area – and that he hears the same sound from you.

• The more times you repeat the above procedure, the more quickly you will toilet-train your puppy. The more often you allow him to go to the toilet in different circumstances (either by accident, or perhaps because you have chosen to allow him to use newspaper indoors during the night), the longer toilet-training will take.

• It is not absolutely necessary to reward successes or at all helpful to punish failures when toilet-training.

• Remember that successful toilet-training is not a battle of wills, but a simple science!

the toilet, but it serves to illustrate the fact that the place in which your puppy relieves himself is as important to him as it is to you. The problem is that, initially, the two of you will have differing views as to what is and what is not a suitable place. Toilet-training is simply the method by which you reach agreement!

FIRST PRINCIPLES

Have you ever heard of Pavlov's dogs? Pavlov was a scientist who succeeded in training his dogs to salivate whenever he rang a bell. As with the actions required to eliminate waste products from the body, the production of saliva is an instinctive response programmed into a dog's brain, and is therefore a subconscious activity.

Normally, you might expect a combination of the sight, smell and perhaps taste of certain food items to trigger salivation, not the ringing of a bell. But Pavlov rang a bell every time he offered his dogs food, and he repeated this again and again. Eventually the sound of the bell became programmed into his dogs' brains, and stimulated salivation even when there was no food.

Toileting by association

As with Pavlov's method, when toilet-training your puppy your aim is to 'program' into his brain a unique combination of sights, smells and perhaps sounds to be associated with his need to go to the toilet. And that is very easy. All you have to do is to make sure that, whenever he is likely to be feeling the desire to go to the toilet, you take him to his designated toileting area. That will take care of the sights and smells. By repeating a simple command – ideally, one that he will not hear at any other time – you will provide a unique sound. Then simply wait until he goes. You may praise your puppy, but there is no need to do so as rewards are not thought to play a part in this kind of learning.

Repeat this process enough times and your puppy will go through a pattern of toileting behaviour whenever he experiences those sights, sounds and smells, even if his bladder or rectum is only partly filled. Getting to this stage will make your life much easier later on, as your puppy will be happy to go to the toilet at your convenience rather than at his own.

Using a puppy crate

Making use of a puppy crate will give you greater control over the times at which your puppy goes to the toilet. If the crate is the correct size and cosy, he will think of it as his nest, and should do all in his power to avoid soiling it. Provided that you do not leave him for too long, shutting the puppy in his crate to sleep, and during the day whenever you cannot

supervise him, will minimize the number of times that he can relieve himself in the wrong places. Get into the habit from the start of taking him to his toileting area as soon as you let him out of his crate.

Your puppy will want to take naps during the day, but do not leave him unsupervised. If you cannot guarantee to be there when he wakes up, you should shut him in his crate. At first, you should plan not to leave him there for more than an hour or so at a time, but this period can be quickly increased.

When you first bring your puppy home, you should be prepared to get up during the night. As he grows older, he should be happy to spend longer in his crate, but you should still be willing to get up if he becomes restless. Use that baby listener! At just three months old, some puppies are quite happy to be left for up to six hours overnight and four hours during the day.

At first, your puppy's crate is likely to be too big for him. This may cause toilet-training problems, as he may sleep at one end of his crate and go to the toilet at the other. In order to prevent this, make the available area smaller by filling up one end of the crate with cardboard boxes.

When will your puppy go to the toilet?

In order to make sure that your puppy experiences the correct training signals as often as possible when he goes to the toilet, you need to know the times when he is likely to want to go. To do this, you must be able to identify the telltale signs that he will show when looking for a place in which to relieve himself. The most obvious signs are those outlined below.

The times
• After eating.
• As soon as he wakes up.
• After any form of excitement, such as exercise, playing games or meeting visitors.
• Whenever he is let out of his puppy crate after a period on his own (see page 75).

The signs
• Sniffing the floor.
• Walking in tight circles with his nose to the ground.
• Adopting a sitting position with his tail held out stiffly.
• Walking with his tail held in the air and the muscles around his anus contracting.

Training your puppy to go to the toilet on command and in a special place will require an appreciation of his natural toileting habits. When he sniffs at the floor in a deliberate way, especially after sleeping or eating (below), it is a telltale sign that he feels the urge to relieve himself. However, at first he will need your help to find his way to his designated toileting area (right).

At any of these times, or whenever you see these signs, take your puppy outside to his toileting area. Repeat your chosen command, and wait until he goes to the toilet. If after five minutes he has not done so, bring him back indoors and keep a very close eye on him. As soon as he shows any of the signs again, take him back outside.

If you bring your puppy home during the winter months, make sure that you have suitable waterproof or warm clothes available. Otherwise, standing outside in the wet and cold during your puppy's toilet-training may be an unpleasant experience!

Dealing with 'accidents'

If your puppy goes to the toilet other than in his designated toileting area in the garden, punishment is pointless. However, saying 'NO' in a stern voice will make you feel better and may break the puppy's concentration. Then take him outside to his proper toileting area as quickly as possible, even if he is still going as you carry him. Do not let him finish what he is doing, and never rub his nose in it.

If you find the end results of an 'accident' that must have happened some time earlier, just get on and clean it up. There is absolutely no point in even showing it to the puppy, as this will be meaningless to him.

Cleaning up 'accidents'

The smells of urine and faeces are natural signals that may stimulate your puppy to go to the toilet, so you should clean up any 'accidents' as soon as possible. Do this very carefully and thoroughly, and remember that your puppy will have a sense of smell that is many times keener than yours.

For hygiene reasons, start by removing the worst of the mess and cleaning up the area with a proper veterinary disinfectant. Then finish off using a cleaning solution that is specifically formulated to remove offending odours. In an emergency when no other cleaning materials are immediately available, a hot solution of biological washing powder makes a good substitute.

How long will toilet-training take?

There is no simple answer to this. It will depend on many factors, including the way your puppy was cared for by his breeder, his age when you collected him, possibly his breed (see above, right), the method that you use, and also the amount of time and effort that you put in. Full toilet-training may take only a few weeks, or could go on for several months.

Professional help

Some breeds of dog seem to be rather more difficult to toilet-train than others. If you experience problems with your puppy, there is no point in blaming either him or yourself, as it could be that you need to adopt a very specific training regime.

If this is the case, you may benefit from the personal assistance of an animal-behaviour expert. Your vet or a veterinary nurse – or perhaps a dog-owning friend who has been through similar problems – should be able to give you a recommendation.

ALTERNATIVE TOILET-TRAINING METHODS

USING A DOG FLAP
Some owners believe that having a dog flap fitted to allow a puppy free access outdoors is the answer, but this is not the case. Your puppy must be toilet-trained by you, and will not be able to work out on his own that he has a special toileting place in the garden – nor may he wish to use it. If you were a puppy and you wanted to go to the toilet, but the weather was cold and wet, would you choose to go outside?

USING NEWSPAPER
A traditional toilet-training method (and one that you may need to employ if you have to leave your puppy for longer periods than he can wait to go to the toilet, or overnight) is to allow a puppy to relieve himself when he wishes, but only in a restricted area on newspaper. However, there are two major flaws in this method. By using paper, you will train the puppy to the sights, sounds and smells of newspaper indoors, and, as you will not always be present when he goes to the toilet, he will not learn your sound command. Toilet-training therefore has to be a much longer process. First you will train your puppy to paper, then you will have to train him again to use his toileting area outdoors.

Your puppy's lifestyle

The quality of your puppy's life will be much more important to him than the quantity of it. After all, like any dog, he will focus on the present and will not worry about the future. For him, life is to be taken day by day. Over the next weeks and months, your puppy is going to become a member of your family and a part of society. He is also going to grow both physically and mentally into an adult dog. Of course, there will be a great deal to learn, but he should also enjoy himself.

A fun life

Your personal circumstances, interests and abilities will all influence the kind of lifestyle that you can give your puppy. For instance, you may be able to offer a Cavalier King Charles spaniel a wonderful quality of life, but you could struggle to give some kinds of terrier enough mental and physical stimulation. That is why choosing the right kind of puppy initially was such an important decision (see pages 42–7).

Freedom versus domesticity

In the wild, a wolf – your puppy's ancestor – leads an unpredictable life. For him, there is no guarantee of a warm bed and a nourishing meal each and every day, and he is constantly stressed and stimulated by the world around him. However, both his body and brain are well-suited to such a lifestyle.

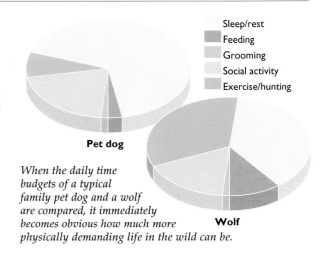

Sleep/rest
Feeding
Grooming
Social activity
Exercise/hunting

Pet dog

Wolf

When the daily time budgets of a typical family pet dog and a wolf are compared, it immediately becomes obvious how much more physically demanding life in the wild can be.

By contrast, pet dogs often lead very routine lives. Many owners feel the need to protect them as though they were helpless babies, even when their dogs are fully grown. Of course, some kinds of pet dog need cosseting because the structure of their bodies is so far removed from what would be required for them to live in the wild. And who knows what domestication has really done to their brains? However, even if your puppy is a regal Pekinese, do not simply assume that he needs – or wishes – to be waited on hand and foot.

Letting your puppy decide

Your puppy is bound to enjoy some experiences more than others. He may, for instance, think that a new game that you have devised is dull, and may simply walk away from you. That is fine: he had the choice, and decided to say no. Equally, if it is raining and your puppy does not want to go for his usual walk, do not force him. It is not obligatory to exercise any dog for a precise number of minutes every day.

Unlike the vast majority of pet dogs, these wolf cubs have to cope with the unpredictable nature of life in the wild. They may not live as long as pet dogs, but their lives will certainly be more active and stimulating.

NEW EXPERIENCES

Throughout his life, you should expose your puppy to new and exciting experiences. Do not go on the same walk at the same time every day, and train your puppy properly so that you can let him off the lead with confidence (see pages 82–5). Some dogs are never allowed to roam freely and to explore when they are out exercising, because their owners are scared that they will never come back. What a shame for those dogs: how they must long to flare their nostrils and feel the wind in their coats. There is more to play, too, than simply throwing a rubber ball for your puppy to fetch: try to introduce variety into all your activities together.

Your puppy is a member of your family, and his health and happiness are your responsibility. The more effort you put into understanding and addressing both his physical and mental needs, the better he will enjoy life.

Keeping fit

The amount of exercise that a dog needs in order to stay fit must relate to his lifestyle (see also pages 92–3). For instance, a racing greyhound will require much more exercise than a pet greyhound to stay on top form, while another breed of dog may have adequate physical exercise just pottering around a large garden.

This is not to say, however, that the latter should not go for walks: the purpose of exercise is not only to exert a dog physically, but also to stimulate his mind. A dog who is taken for very regular but dull walks may be no more physically fit than a dog who has more exciting and interesting walks less frequently, supplemented by plenty of games and play at home, and mentally he will be much worse off.

Creating variety

Be prepared to break with tradition, and dare to be a different kind of dog-owner. Plan a full, varied and fun life for your puppy. Feeding him a good diet, giving him somewhere to rest his head and taking him for two walks around the block every day will keep him reasonably fit and healthy. But would he rather swap a walk for a fun game in your garden? Perhaps more stimulating walks taken less often would suit him better. When appropriate, give your puppy the freedom to make a few decisions for himself. Most of us would agree that our dogs do not live as long as we would like, so it is even more important that they get the most from the short time that they have with us.

First lessons

Most puppies are unable to learn complex tasks before they are about six months old, but they are usually quick to grasp simple human commands from a very young age. You should therefore start training your puppy to be well-behaved as soon as you bring him home.

Training is not simply a matter of organizing formal lessons: your puppy's classroom is the world he lives in, and he will learn all kinds of new skills throughout his waking hours. He will not simply switch off and wait for his teacher to turn up! Without your guidance, he will adopt bad as well as good behaviour. For this reason, rather than allocating set times each day for training, you will be more likely to produce a well-mannered puppy if you teach him desirable skills and behaviour as and when the opportunities arise.

PUPPY PLAYGROUPS

Puppy playgroups are now run in association with many good vet centres. By attending one of these as soon as your puppy has completed his primary-vaccination course (see page 121), you will begin to learn the first principles of training that you can put

Puppy playgroups are fun, but they also have a serious side. You will learn a great deal about dog healthcare and training, and your puppy will broaden his social horizons.

into practice at home. Your time there will also help to improve your understanding of dog behaviour and body language (see pages 36–9), so that you become more confident about handling and interacting with your puppy. In turn, by meeting other puppies and their owners, your puppy will have the opportunity to broaden his horizons and become more familiar with the many different kinds of people, animals and objects that he will encounter during his life.

What are puppy playgroups for?

Despite their name, puppy playgroups are not simply an excuse for a gang of puppies to have a fun time and for their owners to have a natter. A good playgroup will offer you and your puppy a structured course of instruction and practical interaction relating to dog behaviour and early training. If possible, all the members of your family should attend.

The precise course content covered by a particular playgroup will obviously depend on the instructor, but your puppy should learn the following from his playgroup sessions.
• How to interact with adults of both sexes, as well as with children.
• How to interact with other puppies and adult dogs.
• How to respond to simple commands.
Ask at your vet centre for details of puppy playgroups held in your area. Look for one that is run by someone with relevant knowledge and experience, who is also a member of a nationally recognized organization such as (in the UK) the Association of Pet Dog Trainers, or the Association of Pet-behaviour Counsellors.

HOW DO PUPPIES LEARN?

Your puppy will learn most of what you teach him via what is called 'instrumental learning'. The basic principle of this is that, if the puppy is immediately rewarded for performing a certain behaviour in response to a particular situation or stimulus, he will be more likely to enact the same behaviour if he encounters that situation again. For example, if he hears you say

'SIT' as he begins to rest his bottom on the ground from a standing position, and you immediately praise him, he will remember the association between the sound you made (the stimulus), his behaviour and the reward. After many repetitions of this procedure, when he hears the sound 'SIT' he will be more likely to park his bottom! Your role in training your puppy is to make sure that the stimulus, the behaviour and the reward all occur at the correct time and in the correct way to ensure that learning takes place.

Giving rewards

The most effective training rewards for your puppy will be those things that he anticipates with eagerness, or makes some effort to obtain. If he is anything like most dogs, he should see the following as major rewards.

• Your attention: praise or petting.
• Food: very small nuggets of a high-quality complete dry puppy food, prepared dog treats and oven-baked pieces of liver are all used by animal-behaviour experts.
• Mental or physical stimulation: examples include being let out into the garden, or having a ball thrown.

To teach her puppy to release his favourite toy, this owner uses a tiny piece of food as a training reward. The puppy is happy to drop the toy on command because he is keen to obtain the food.

WHAT MAKES A GOOD REWARD?

Be sure to use a variety of rewards when training your puppy. By doing so, you should avoid the situation in which he suddenly fails to respond to your commands because his normal reward is unavailable, or because he is bored with the same 'treat'. Whatever rewards you use, they must all be seen by your puppy as such.

Some dog-owners worry about using food rewards. Don't. Food is often the most effective reward for many puppies. Just make sure that, if you use anything other than a part of his normal food, you give only very small pieces so that you do not upset the nutritional balance or calorie level of your puppy's overall diet.

A reward must be given at exactly the same time that your puppy carries out the desired behaviour, as a delay of even one second can weaken its effect. At first, when starting to train your puppy, reward him every time he responds correctly. However, once he has mastered something you should only reward him occasionally. Dogs do 'unlearn' trained actions, but research shows that types of behaviour rewarded only occasionally are the least likely to be forgotten.

What about punishment?

You may think that, if your puppy learns his good behaviour through associating desirable actions with pleasant rewards, the best way to prevent bad behaviour is to ensure that he associates undesirable actions with unpleasant punishments. Wrong: the opposite of a reward is in fact the absence of a reward. For example, if your puppy is about to chew the leg of your favourite antique chair, distract him. If it makes you feel better, saying 'NO' in a stern voice will do. If you go to the puppy and pull him away from the chair, he is likely to see your attention as a reward, even if you are angry with him.

As soon as you have broken your puppy's concentration from a distance, call him to you and then praise him for responding quickly. It will stay in his mind subsequently that he was rewarded for returning to you.

The main point to remember in training lessons is to concentrate on rewarding good behaviour. Whenever possible, try to ignore bad behaviour.

Basic training

Not every owner needs a dog who is as well-trained as an obedience champion. However, what every owner would like – and has a responsibility to create – is a dog who is well-behaved in public, and safe with other people and animals.

By teaching your puppy to respond well to the basic commands outlined in the following pages, you will initiate that process. You are bigger than your puppy and you will probably be able to make him do what you wish, but successful training is about encouraging him to respond to the commands because he chooses to do so. Your puppy should be a keen participant in training, not a reluctant conscript.

Command words

One word must have one meaning. Everyone in your family should know all the commands that you use with your puppy, what they mean and when to use them (for example, if 'SIT' and 'DOWN' are separate commands, no-one should tell him to 'SIT DOWN'). The words that you choose are up to you, but each command must be simple, distinctive and consistent.

The re-call 'COME'

'SIT', 'STAY' and 'LIE' can all wait. The first lesson that you need to teach your puppy is to 'COME' when he is called, so that you will be confident enough to let him run free. Given the dangers and hazards that exist outdoors, it is possible that a quick response to this command could save his life.

1 Ask someone to hold your puppy. Get down to the puppy's level, and attract his attention by holding a food reward in front of his nose. Then walk a few paces backwards and squat down.

TRAINING TIP

When your puppy comes to you, avoid the temptation to seize him by his collar, to hug him passionately or to stroke his head furiously. He will not like this, and will probably jump back or wriggle away so that he can keep his focus on the reward in your hand.

2 While the puppy is still concentrating on you and on the food reward, call his name, followed by the command 'COME' (your assistant should be primed to release the puppy immediately). Keep repeating your puppy's name and the command in an excited voice, and smile and open out your arms to welcome him.

3 When he arrives, praise him. After a few seconds, gently take hold of his collar and feed him the reward. Praise him again, then let him wander away.

Hand signals

Dogs are experts at interpreting our body language (see pages 37–9). The use of individual and clearly distinguishable actions on your part – such as specific hand signals that are strictly associated with certain commands – will therefore help your puppy to learn.

Concentration

Before carrying out any training task, make sure that your puppy is calm and that he is concentrating on you. He should understand that, when he hears his name, something good is going to happen to him, so never use his name in vain. As soon as he looks at you, reward him appropriately (see page 81). Your puppy will not have a very long attention span when you begin training him, but you should always try to finish a session while he is still concentrating.

If possible, begin training sessions in the safety of your own garden, and make sure that there are no distractions. Right from the start, you should do everything necessary to convince your puppy that, wherever you both are, you are more important than anything else that may be going on around you.

The command 'SIT'

This command is a relatively easy one to teach, as it is something that your puppy does naturally all the time. Whenever he sits when he is with you, use your command word, even if you are not actually intending to train him. The more he associates your command with his action, the better.

2 Hold the food reward by his nose, then move your hand as if trying to put the food on his head. Your puppy should follow your hand with his nose. In a standing position, 'star-gazing' in this way is awkward for him, so he should automatically sit. As he begins to bend his hindlegs, keep repeating the command 'SIT'.

1 Approach your puppy, kneel down and attract his attention by saying his name. As he looks at you, show him that you have a food reward in your hand.

TRAINING TIPS

- Do not move your hand too quickly, or your puppy will simply walk backwards.

- Keep your hand low to prevent him from trying to jump up for the reward.

- Introduce an appropriate hand signal as soon as you and your puppy are familiar with this exercise.

3 As soon as the puppy sits down, give him the reward in your hand.

The command 'DOWN'

This straightforward lesson should follow on fairly easily once your puppy is familiar with the command to sit (see page 83). Once again, use your command word whenever he lies down, even voluntarily.

1 Approach your puppy, kneel down and attract his attention by saying his name. As he looks at you, ask him to sit and show him that you have a food reward in your hand.

2 Move your hand containing the reward from the puppy's nose towards the ground, aiming for a position just between his paws. He should remain sitting but follow your hand with his nose.

3 Move your hand backwards and forwards on the ground to keep him interested. In an attempt to get his nose and mouth closer to the reward, your puppy should lie down voluntarily. As he starts to bend his forelegs, keep repeating the command 'DOWN'.

TRAINING TIPS

• If your puppy stands up instead of lying down, conceal the food reward and start again.

• If the procedure described does not seem to work, an alternative method is for you to sit on the floor with your legs bent to make a small tunnel. Hold the food reward in your hand between your legs, so that your puppy has to 'commando-crawl' under your legs to reach your hand. Use the command 'DOWN' and then release the reward, as above.

PUPPY-TRAINING CLASSES

You may at some stage need specific training advice, although many of your questions should be answered at your puppy playgroup (see page 80). Before attending a puppy-training class, first go to visit the class without your puppy. Take note of your first impressions: training should be fun for both dogs and humans! You should also ask yourself the following questions.

• Are the classes small enough to allow you and your puppy to receive personal attention?

• Will all the members of your family be able to attend the classes on a regular basis?

• Does the training use reward-based methods?

• Is the instructor knowledgeable about dog behaviour as well as experienced in training? Is he or she firm but kind, or an authoritative disciplinarian?

• Is the class designed for pet dogs, or is it actually more of a competition-obedience class?

The command 'STAY'

Teaching a puppy to stay is another important facet of basic training, but one that many owners overlook to their cost. As with the re-call (see page 82), obeying a command to 'STAY' could save your puppy's life.

TRAINING TIPS

• Remain still when first teaching this command, as your puppy may perceive any movement as a signal to move.

• Choose a release word so that your puppy knows when he can move. 'OKAY' or 'FINISH' are examples.

OUT IN PUBLIC

If you do not have an enclosed garden, you may have to train your puppy in a more public place. If so, be sure not to take him there until at least one week after his primary-vaccination course (see page 121).

At first, for safety's sake, you should have something connecting you to your puppy's collar at all times: an extending lead is ideal, but a light rope will do. Never pull your puppy by this. When he moves towards you, simply take up the slack with your free hand.

Your first training session in public off the lead should be in an open area that is well away from any major hazards such as roads.

1 With your puppy on his lead, ask him to sit, then reward him as normal. Wait beside him, and ask him to 'STAY'. If he remains sitting, reward him after a few seconds. If he moves, return him to a sitting position and try again.

2 Gradually increase the time between asking the puppy to 'SIT' and 'STAY', and reward him when he stays put. Repeat the exercise until he will remain sitting for several minutes, then practise using a specific hand signal.

3 Repeat the exercise, but step away from the puppy so that he has to wait at a distance from you. Develop his new ability to stay in one place by moving around him, repeating the appropriate verbal command and hand signal.

Walking on a loose lead: 'WALK'

Many owners experience problems with this skill, as they find that their puppies either sit down and refuse to move, or that they pull. However, you should avoid these problems if you think carefully about what it feels like to be on the other end of a lead!

1 For this training exercise, use a fixed lead of 1–2 m (3–6 ft) in length. Attract your puppy's attention, attach the lead and then encourage him to come and stand next to you (it does not matter which side this is, provided that it is consistent). Offer your puppy a food reward when he does so.

Adjust the length of the lead so that, with your puppy at your side, it is slack but not dangling on the ground. Hold your end close to your chest to keep it at this length. Attract your puppy's attention again using his name, then say 'WALK' and move forwards.

2 If the lead becomes taut, stop walking so that your puppy comes to an abrupt halt, then encourage him back into his former position at your side. When he is calm and you have his attention, repeat the command 'WALK' and move off. Reward him with your praise as he trots along on a loose lead.

GROWING OLDER

As with humans, adolescence in dogs is a time for extending their horizons. This may include an element of rebelliousness: for example, even a previously very obedient dog may begin to ignore the re-call command. A firm but kind regime will teach your older puppy to continue to respect you and your family.

Further training

Your puppy's basic, reward-based training should be continued, not only at a weekly class but at home and on walks as well. Training can also be incorporated into play sessions, by simple methods such as asking your puppy to sit before you throw his ball. Obedience to these basic principles will ensure that he continues to develop into a well-mannered companion.

Meeting other dogs

During adolescence, your puppy will become much more confident and boisterous. He will no longer be behaving as a puppy, and will not be treated as such by other dogs. It is therefore important that he learns the behaviour that is appropriate to an adult.

This may entail the occasional 'telling off' from older dogs but, as this is the natural course of events, you should not be worried and you should not prevent your puppy interacting with other dogs from fear that they may pick a fight with him. However, do avoid any dogs who are not under their owners' control, and closely supervise any meetings. If a strange dog becomes aggressive, lead your puppy away.

Adolescent behaviour

Play between dogs – particularly adolescents – can be an energetic, noisy affair that may easily be mistaken for fighting. If your puppy is 'playing' with other dogs and you think that things may be getting out of hand, look at the dogs' body language. Wagging tails, bouncy behaviour and 'play-bows' (with the dogs' front ends on the ground and bottoms in the air) are all sure signs that a game is in progress.

Your puppy may also take a renewed interest in things about which he was nonchalant when younger.

Some puppies are easier to train than others; equally, some owners are better dog-trainers than others. If you experience problems when training your puppy, you and he may well benefit from the personal attention of a suitably qualified pet-dog trainer or animal-behaviour expert.

Rabbits and squirrels may suddenly become exciting to chase, and he may also begin to look on cyclists and other animals as fair game. Do not give up on the good work that you did earlier, to teach your puppy to be controlled in such situations. Tell him to 'LEAVE' when he is about to interact with something that you wish him to ignore, and reward him for staying calm.

One step at a time

Periods of sleep will be interspersed with longer periods of activity, and your older puppy will need more exercise and mental stimulation as he grows up. Basic commands need to be practised throughout the day and new 'tricks' taught to keep him stimulated.

However, do not push your puppy too fast, as this can lead to a reduction in confidence as well as to an unwillingness to perform. It is worth noting that guide dogs and sheepdogs do not learn the more difficult aspects of their jobs until they are one year old.

Out and about

One week after your puppy has completed his primary-vaccination course (see page 121), he can begin exploring the great outdoors. He has a lot to learn about the kind of world that he lives in, and becoming accustomed to new sights, sounds and smells is all part of growing up. You too will have to cope with many new experiences: for instance, your puppy will be an extra passenger in your car or on the bus, and road safety will mean nothing to him.

Over the next days and weeks, you should aim to familiarize your puppy with all the objects, animals and environments with which he is likely to come into contact when he is away from home. He may take some new experiences in his stride, while others may frighten or over-excite him. How will you cope with his reactions? The way that you behave towards him will affect the way he reacts to an experience when he encounters it the next time.

Fear

If a pack of dogs is running towards your puppy it may be sensible to pick him up to avoid conflict, but do not do so unless you think it absolutely necessary, as he must learn to cope when he is on the ground.

If he cowers when a large lorry passes by, ignore him or just talk to him. Stroking and fussing him will simply reward his reaction: dogs do not understand the concept of reassurance. However, avoid dragging your puppy along as if nothing has happened, or he will feel that going out is an uncomfortable experience. When he has composed himself, walk forwards and encourage him to follow close to you. As soon as he is happy and confident again, reward him with praise.

You will quickly become aware of what frightens your puppy, and you must make a special effort to introduce him to these things gradually. For instance, if he dislikes lorries, find a road where they pass further away from the pavement. Reward confident and happy behaviour and ignore fearful reactions, and – with a little time and patience – you should be able to move him nearer and nearer to the objects of which he was frightened. Remember that in any new situation your puppy will look to you for leadership. If you are at all anxious, he will be more so; if you are confident, he should follow your example.

Over-excitement

In certain situations your puppy may become over-excited, pulling and barking at something he has seen: perhaps an unfamiliar animal such as a horse. There is nothing you can do there and then, except to move him away and try to distract him.

From this point onwards, you will need to keep a sharp look-out for horses. If you see one before your puppy does so, make sure that you have firm control of him and then move a little closer. Stop at a safe distance, where your puppy can see the horse but has not become agitated. Attract your puppy's attention, ask him to sit (see page 83) and then reward him in the normal way. Keep his attention, continue to praise him and then walk away. The next time, move a little closer and repeat the procedure.

Calmness and confidence

Excellent: talk to your puppy and reward him with praise for his nonchalant behaviour.

USING POOPER-SCOOPERS

Your puppy may go to the toilet in the most embarrassing places. However, by clearing up after him straight away you will prove that you are not only a dog-lover, but a responsible owner.

Pooper-scoopers are hygienic and very easy to use. Place what you have collected in a special bin, or – if none is provided where you walk with your puppy – take what you have scooped home with you for disposal.

THE OUTDOOR CODE

• Keep your puppy under control at all times.
• Keep him on a lead near main roads or livestock.
• Avoid allowing your puppy to go to the toilet on pavements or lawns, or in open spaces where the public roam or children play. Always clean up after him.
• In the country, shut gates behind you and keep to signed paths.
• Be vigilant in supervising your puppy near water.

IN THE CAR

It must be a very strange experience for a dog to see the world whizzing by when he looks down at his feet and they are not moving. Many dogs take cars in their stride, but others are not such good travellers. You should aim to accustom your puppy to your car from a very young age by regularly allowing him to climb into it, even before he is allowed out (see page 121). If he gets in confidently, praise and reward him; if he needs some encouragement, feed him in the car.

Next, bring the car to life by turning on the engine, and deal with your puppy's reactions as you would do if he experienced something new when out and about (see opposite). Even before he has completed his first vaccinations, take your puppy for short trips in the car, and reward him with a game when you are safely back at home. Gradually increase the distance that you travel until he is completely confident.

If your puppy suffers from motion sickness, feed him well in advance of travelling, and ask your vet for medication if necessary.

Car safety

In the event of an accident at just 30 miles (48 km) per hour, an average labrador retriever, unrestrained on the back seat, is likely to be hurled forwards with such force that he will take on the equivalent weight of an adult elephant. He may be seriously injured, or killed, and could also kill whoever is sitting in front of him.

There are a number of different options to keep your puppy safe in the car.

Car cage • This can be used in either a hatchback or an estate car and, in my view, is the best car-safety option available. Look in any dog magazine for specialist suppliers.

Dog-guard • This can also be used in a hatchback or an estate car. I would recommend a guard with a grille design rather than a tubular one. Make sure that it is suitable for your make of car, and fit it correctly. (Note: if you use a dog-guard rather than a full car cage, take great care that your puppy does not jump out when you lift up the tailgate, before you can get hold of him. Teach him to 'STAY' where he is until you invite him to get out.)

Car harness • This is suitable for any type of car, and attaches to one of the human seatbelts. Make sure that a harness fits your puppy correctly, and that it is properly secured before you set off.

Carrying basket • This is suitable for a smaller dog. The basket must be properly secured so that it cannot move around (see pages 70–1).

Dog harnesses such as this one are designed to be attached to a car seatbelt. They are available in a number of different sizes, and are also adjustable to ensure a perfect fit.

Travelling tips

• For long journeys, take a supply of food and water in case of hold-ups. Do not forget your puppy's bowl, as well as a tin-opener if you use canned food. It is easily done, believe me!

• Make regular breaks for your puppy to stretch his legs and relieve himself. Choose proper resting places with appropriate facilities, and clean up after him.

• Always keep a supply of pooper-scoopers, a spare lead and a toy in your car, as well as a basic first-aid kit (make sure that you know how to use this).

• If you need to stop overnight, make arrangements for your puppy in advance.

• Avoid feeding your puppy just before you leave, and ensure that he has been to the toilet before you set off.

WARNING

On a warm day, the temperature in a car can quickly rise to over 49°C (120°F). A dog left inside will pant frantically to try to keep cool, but he is likely to be well on the way to heatstroke. In a short time he may be dead. In the UK and elsewhere, people who leave their dogs in the car in warm weather may be asked to justify their actions to an animal-welfare inspector.

Exercise and play

To stay mentally and physically fit, your puppy will need to exert both his body and his brain. Exercise and play are not totally different activities: a well-chosen walk will be as stimulating for his senses and his mind as it will be demanding for his body, while good toys will keep him entertained and active at the same time.

Planning the right sort of activities for your puppy is very important, but – once you have created an activity plan for him – do not stick by it rigidly for the rest of his life. Keep thinking up new activities, and give your puppy the freedom to choose those that he finds most stimulating. There are only three points to remember: variety, variety and variety!

Where to exercise your puppy

At first, because of the risk of disease, your puppy's exercise and play activities should be limited to your house and garden, but once he completes his initial

Roaming freely in a safe and natural environment is not only mentally stimulating but provides excellent physical exercise for dog and owner alike.

vaccination course (see page 121) he should regularly venture further afield.

Different activities are obviously better-suited to certain environments. You may not have sufficient room in your garden to throw a Frisbee, for instance, while throwing a ball when out walking in long grass is a sure way of losing it. Try to visit a diverse range of environments with your puppy, such as built-up areas, open fields, woodland and – if you are lucky enough to live near the sea – the beach.

Why exercise and play with your puppy?

• To develop a strong relationship with him. All the people who live with him should be actively involved.
• To improve his co-ordination and athletic skills.
• To reinforce his training in a practical setting.
• To keep his body toned, his mind alert and his reflexes sharp.
• To allow him to express natural behaviour, such as that involved in scent trailing and hunting.
• To make his life – and yours – more fun.

ACTIVITY OPTIONS

We tend to be very traditional about what we consider to be essential exercise for dogs, but different kinds of dog prefer – and are suited to – different activities. A breed such as a border collie, a dalmatian or a golden retriever will need plenty of opportunities to stretch its legs, whereas a tiny Yorkshire terrier does not have much in the way of legs to stretch. The totally distorted shape of a British bulldog's face means that he physically cannot get air in and out of his lungs quickly enough to have any chance of keeping up with his more athletic cousins.

Of course, this does not mean that a Yorkshire terrier or a British bulldog should not be given the stimulation and enjoyment of regular short walks, but jogging definitely will nott suit them! You should aim to offer your puppy a balance of activities. It does not matter if some days are more active than others, but every day should be full of fun.

Walks on the lead

Lead walks on pavements or other hard surfaces are good opportunities to reinforce basic training. They will also familiarize your puppy with traffic, bicycles and other everyday hustle and bustle, and will help to keep his nails in good condition.

Walks off the lead

Off-lead exercise is essential for your puppy as soon as you have perfected his re-call training (see page 82). Make sure that at gates and other obstacles you are in control of him, or he may try something dangerously acrobatic.

Remember that, when running off the lead, your puppy may cover many times the distance that you walk. If he is extremely energetic, only let him run free for short periods at a time (see pages 92–3).

Swimming

This is excellent exercise for a puppy, and puts less strain on bones and joints than most land-based activities. Any water should be safe and relatively clean, and not fast-flowing. Always check that your puppy has an easy and shallow exit route from water.

Games

These can be played almost anywhere, and should be mentally stimulating for your puppy. As time goes by, you and he will create many new games, but the following are just a few ideas to start you off.

Fetch the toy • Some puppies gain endless amusement from this; others need more encouragement. If your puppy is reluctant to come back to you when he has found the toy, have another in your hand to attract his attention. Odd-shaped toys are fun because they bounce unpredictably. Fetch games are a good way of reinforcing re-call training (see page 82).

Find the toy • Hiding a toy and helping your puppy to find it will test his senses and your ingenuity skills. Avoid making this too difficult at first, and make sure that your puppy finds the toy in the end.

Find the person • Ask a friend to hold your puppy while you hide with one of his toys. Remain hidden and start to call your puppy. As he gets nearer, call to him less often so that he has to use his nose and eyes as well as his ears. When he finds you, let him know how pleased you are.

Chew the toy • Your puppy will pick up an object in his mouth simply to play with it, but he will also learn about its weight and texture. If he is teething,

Dogs who enjoy swimming find it very difficult not to get their feet wet whenever the opportunity arises. However, you should train your puppy to remain on dry land until you have assessed whether it is safe for him to dive in.

chewing on the object may relieve the discomfort. He may even practise his natural feeding skills: shaking an object ensures that it is dead, while pulling it apart reduces it into pieces that would be small enough to swallow. Because of this tendency, any toys that you give your puppy should be as near-indestructible as possible.

Tug • Tugging at an object to try to win it is also natural behaviour, but this game can get out of hand. Make sure that it is you who always starts and finishes the game, and teach your puppy to drop the object on command (see below).

GAME RULES

When playing with toys, you must teach your puppy to give them up on command. Use a simple command such as 'DROP' or 'GIVE', and reward him for obeying (see page 81). Once he has learned the command, keep practising it as part of your everyday play together.

Games to avoid

When you play with your puppy, do not inadvertently encourage him to act in a way that, at any other time, you would take as misbehaviour.

Jumping up • If your puppy jumps up at you when you are about to throw one of his toys for him to fetch, throwing it will serve as a reward for that behaviour. Your puppy will then be more likely to jump up at you again, not only when you are playing fetch but also when it is time for his dinner or when he wants your attention.

Rough-and-tumble games • These will encourage your puppy to see you as a toy: he will not understand why you become upset when he sinks his teeth into you for fun.

Snatching objects • Your puppy may love to snatch something and then run away in the hope of being chased. This can be very amusing until he steals something valuable or dangerous, and you need to get hold of him quickly.

Encouraging good behaviour

Puppies are very good at learning the behaviour that is quickest to attract our attention. Make sure that good behaviour gets a much bigger and better response than bad behaviour, or you will actually be encouraging your puppy to misbehave. Always reward him when he sits on command, lies down quietly and refrains from jumping up.

If he barks at you, or runs around the room madly biting at the furniture and stealing objects, say 'NO' in a stern voice and then ignore him.

WARNING

Throwing a stick for your puppy to bring back can be a dangerous game. When the stick lands, it may fall so that your puppy tries to pick it up by one end. If he has run towards it, he may misjudge its length and the stick could pierce the back of his throat. Your puppy could die as a result of such a wound.

Many dogs adore playing hide-and-seek games with their owners. Even if your puppy cannot see you, his highly refined sense of smell should enable him to track you down quickly despite your best efforts to keep yourself concealed.

How much exercise?

The precise activity regime that suits both you and your puppy will depend on many factors, including his stature, the type of dog he is, his temperament and his age, as well as on your physical abilities and the time that you have available for him.

The responsibility for planning, monitoring and adjusting your puppy's activity regime is up to you. If you are in any doubt, seek advice: speak to other experienced owners, to the instructor at your puppy playgroup (see page 80), or to your vet or a veterinary nurse. This is important, because puppies of some of the larger and giant breeds may be prone to specific developmental orthopaedic problems, and may benefit from a carefully restricted exercise plan.

Avoid allowing your puppy to engage in too much physical activity when he is young. If you are in any way unhappy about your puppy's apparent ability to exercise, or you spot any of the following signs, contact your vet centre for advice.

• He often stops to rest during a play session, or out on a walk.

• He has difficulty in keeping up with you on walks.

• He continues panting for a long period after exercise or play, even when the weather is cool.

• He finds it difficult to fall asleep and is restless after exercise or play.

• He is stiff or limping when he gets up having rested after exercise.

• He is stiff or limping on exercise.

• His legs begin to look bowed.

• He yelps when you pick him up or move any of his joints.

• He is suddenly reluctant to participate in his normal activities.

Equally, watch out for the following signs that your puppy is under-exerting himself either mentally or physically.

• He becomes overweight.

• He is excessively destructive or attention-seeking. He may simply be bored stiff!

Suitable toys

• Only buy products that are both properly packaged and labelled with full instructions for their use.

• Assume that any toy will be destructible: always monitor how your puppy gets on with a new toy before leaving him unsupervised.

• Some dog toys are specifically designed to stimulate natural instincts. In general I have found these excellent, even though they can be a little expensive.

• Offer toys in rotation to maintain your puppy's interest.

• If you use any toys to play 'fetch' on water, make sure that they float!

Playing 'fetch' games with your puppy will help you to reinforce his re-call training (see page 82).

FUN WITH YOUR OLDER PUPPY

As your puppy grows older, you should be able to tackle progressively more adventurous activities. However, his exercise should still be controlled until he is fully grown: this may be as early as six months if he is a small dog, or over a year if he is a larger breed. When he is mature, you can look forward to becoming involved in exciting dog sports such as agility and flyball. Believe me, if you get into dog agility your weekends will never be the same again.

Leaving your puppy

Although your puppy is a pack animal and would rather be with you 24 hours a day, there will be many times when he is left on his own. This may be either at night or during the day when you are still within earshot, or when you go out and he is the only one left in the house.

There will also be times when you must go away for longer periods without your puppy: perhaps at short notice due to an unexpected work commitment, or when you go on holiday and are unable to take him.

LEAVING YOUR PUPPY ON HIS OWN

You will spend a lot of time teaching your puppy how to behave when you are with him. Do not assume that, when he is alone, he will always switch off and go to sleep. You and he should regularly spend time apart, not just at night-time but also during the day.

Separation anxiety

It is extremely important that – right from the start – your puppy learns how to cope and behave well when separated from you and the rest of his family, or you could find that he never learns to manage without you.

Separation anxiety, as it is known, is one of the most common behavioural problems suffered by pet dogs. Some may exhibit symptoms of anxiety, or just become plain mischievous; others may 'forget' their toilet-training, become destructive or bark, whine or howl in their owners' absence. Once established, separation anxiety is treatable, but it is much easier and also more sensible to prevent its occurrence at the start.

Basic separation training

I have already recommended that to toilet-train your puppy quickly, and to prevent him from coming to harm, you should consider putting him in a puppy crate when you cannot supervise him (see page 52). If you have taken my advice, your puppy may already be quite accustomed to being on his own.

However, if he still dislikes his own company, or he has not yet experienced being alone during the day because you diligently watch over his every move, your puppy will benefit from some basic separation training. Even if you have no plans ever to leave him alone, you never know what the future may hold.

Several times during the day, make sure that you and your puppy are separated by a closed door. This should not just be when he is sleepy: if he is to learn

to cope alone, he needs to be awake. Leave him with something interesting to occupy his mind, such as a safe toy. This should be a 'special' toy that he will only have when he is alone. At first, rub a small amount of a food item such as cream cheese or butter inside the toy, if you think it will help to amuse your puppy. If he normally experiences plenty of noise in your house, he may feel less lonely if he has a radio nearby.

After shutting the door behind you, do not make a deliberate effort to be quiet but simply get on with whatever you were doing. Initially, leave your puppy on his own for periods of just a few minutes, but not for exactly the same length of time on each occasion: your return should be unpredictable. Provided that he

TEACHING INDEPENDENCE

With patience and practice, your puppy should soon start to learn that separation from you on occasions is the price of your company at all other times.

Even when you are with your puppy, do not give him your full attention every time he asks for it. If you are reading and in the middle of a good bit, ignore him. Treating your puppy in this way every now and again will make him less dependent on you.

is not bored with the toy, he should still be quiet when you go back to him. This is important, because if you appear when he has begun to whine or bark your presence will reward this behaviour, not the fact that he was quiet earlier. If he is quiet when you return, remove the toy and praise him, then reward him with a game.

When you are sure that your puppy can cope happily with short periods on his own, vary things a little. Leave him his toy, but do not always doctor it with food; or give him a different toy (his special toy will not last for ever, so he should not become dependent on it). Next, increase the length of time you are apart, and make some separations longer than others: work towards a maximum of four hours.

HOME ALONE

Sooner rather than later, you must leave your puppy at home on his own. Even if you do not really have to go out, force yourself, and do so every day. You must be able to trust your puppy, and he must experience you shutting the door behind you. The way in which you leave the house, and your behaviour towards your puppy before you go, are all-important.

When leaving your puppy, ensure that the areas to which he has access are safe and that he has a few home comforts, such as a toy and the sound of a radio playing nearby.

Tips on leaving your puppy

• Half an hour before leaving your puppy, pay him much less attention than normal. You can actually be quite offhand with him. This will help to smooth the change-over from your presence to your absence.
• Avoid lingering goodbyes. Settle your puppy in his bed quickly and efficiently, make sure that he has his toy and any other creature comforts, and then set off.
• Be unpredictable, so that your puppy cannot guess what is happening: sometimes leave the house wearing indoor clothes, sometimes put on your coat but do not leave, and sometimes put on your coat in front of him. Do not always leave by the same door. We tend to do the same things in the same order when leaving the house, but try to break your old habits. Vary the time at which you leave, or you will soon realize that your puppy has a very good built-in clock.

• Try to fool your puppy that you may still be around in the house. If you think it may help, leave a radio on, make sure that the heating will not switch off as soon as you go, or leave the dishwasher on. Some dirty washing in a clothes basket will remind him of you!
• When you return, open the door and take a deep breath. If the puppy has been well-behaved, praise him; if not, do not punish him, but simply ignore him or act in a normal way.

IF YOU HAVE PROBLEMS

Despite your best efforts, your puppy may not cope well when separated from you. If this is the case, don't worry. Speak to your vet or a veterinary nurse: he or she should be able to put you in touch with a dog-behaviour expert who can offer you specific advice.

Going away without your puppy

There will be times when you have to go away without your puppy. For instance, it could be inappropriate for him to accompany you on a foreign summer holiday, to an important wedding or on a murder-mystery weekend break in a city hotel.

Whether you are going away for just a day or two, or for several weeks, you will need to make suitable arrangements for your puppy's care. One option is to ask a friend or relative to look after him. Alternatively, like the majority of dog-owners, you could arrange for him to stay in a suitable boarding kennel. And then, of course, there are puppy-sitters!

BOARDING KENNELS

Your puppy will appreciate the time and effort that you put into finding a really good kennels for him. What is more, you will be able to go away happy in the knowledge that he is in safe hands. Even if you do not intend to put your puppy into kennels, you never know how your circumstances may change, so you must be prepared. Sudden, unexpected work commitments or illness may mean that you need to board your puppy at short notice.

Planning ahead

Choose the boarding kennels that you would like to use (see below), and make sure that your puppy can familiarize himself there well in advance (see above, right). If possible, book early, as the best kennels are often busy, especially over major holiday periods.

Before going to kennels your puppy will need to be fully up-to-date with his main vaccinations, and may need an additional injection to help protect him from a condition called kennel cough (see pages 120–1).

Choosing the right kennels

1 Make a shortlist of just a few boarding kennels, based on recommendations from the staff at your vet centre and from other dog-owners. The kennels should be based within a reasonable distance from your home, but avoid concentrating solely on those that are really convenient: going a little further afield may put much better kennels within reach.

2 Ideally, you should then make arrangements to visit all the boarding kennels on your list. If the owners of an establishment say that they do not allow inspection visits, scrub them from your list.

GETTING USED TO BOARDING KENNELS

Experiencing kennelling early in life will help your puppy to learn that he has nothing to fear. Take him to your chosen kennels once or twice for visits: a quick potter about will enable him to become acquainted with the sights, sounds and smells of the place, and to associate them with pleasant feelings such as petting by the staff. After visiting the kennels, board your puppy there for an afternoon and, later on, for an overnight stay. In this way he should learn that you will return.

When you leave your puppy, do so with little fuss, and make sure that he is surrounded by familiar and favourite things that remind him of home.

3 At each boarding kennels, ask to see the owners' licence (this should be displayed in a prominent position). When looking around, judge for yourself the conditions under which the guests are kept. It does not matter if each kennel is fairly spartan as you should be able to bring your puppy's own creature comforts, but the whole environment should be clean and warm, and feel fresh and airy. Dogs should have individual exercise runs, and the kennels should also offer good facilities for outdoor exercise and play.

Check that there are isolation facilities available for sick dogs, and find out what the owners would do if your puppy were unwell, or if your return were delayed for any reason. Make sure that the property is well-fenced, and that both the security and the fire-prevention measures are adequate. Someone should be on the kennel premises 24 hours a day and, ideally, anyone on duty should have basic first-aid skills in case of an emergency.

The owners of good kennels should in turn wish to know everything about your puppy, including his particular likes and dislikes, his diet regime, whether or not he has been in boarding kennels before, whether he has any special medical needs, and which are his favourite toys.

4 Most important of all, value your first impressions about the place and about the staff who work there. Will you be happy to leave your puppy with them, and, knowing your puppy as well as you do, will he be happy to stay? If there is a visitors' book, read it. Be suspicious of any torn-out pages!

Items to take to kennels

The following is a checklist of the items to take when your puppy goes to boarding kennels.
• An adequate supply of any special food items, along with a clear and comprehensive diet sheet.
• Your puppy's vaccination card, along with the name and contact details of your vet centre (see below).
• Some of your puppy's bedding, and a selection of his favourite toys.
• Instructions as to what to do in the event of an emergency (see below), including your contact details while you are away.
• Precise instructions relating to any special medical or general-care procedures that your puppy will need

When you take your puppy to boarding kennels, make sure that you have all his bits and pieces with you (see left and below), and try to avoid any long and lingering farewells.

(you should make sure that you have the kennel owners' agreement in advance to carry these out).
• Written details of any of your puppy's particular likes and dislikes, together with any special commands or actions that he understands. These will help the kennel staff to look after him as well as possible and to make him feel at home.

Alternatives to boarding kennels

You could ask a neighbour or relative to look after your puppy while you are away, but try not to put anyone under pressure to do so – it is a very big responsibility to look after someone else's dog.

If you really do not want to put your puppy into kennels, it may be worth considering employing someone to live in your house while you are away. If you have a number of animals, this may in fact be the most cost-effective solution. Make sure that anyone you use gets on well with your puppy, has excellent references and is properly trained. Some puppy-sitters have a lot of experience and are very trustworthy.

SENSIBLE PRECAUTIONS

If your puppy is unwell or injured while you are away, it may be difficult for the kennel-owners to contact you. It is therefore a good idea to inform the staff at your vet centre that you are going away, and to advise them of what your wishes would be if your puppy were to require medical assistance in your absence. Leave full contact details for the centre with the kennel-owners.

Taking your puppy away with you

Some of the best holidays I have ever taken have been with my dog, and, for many families, holidays are one of the few times when everyone – including the dog – can be together. But do not just pack up this weekend and head off into the countryside: you will need to make some arrangements in advance.

In addition, if you decide to visit another country, it may be difficult to take your puppy with you. For example, having left the UK, a puppy must spend six months in quarantine kennels when he arrives home. Your puppy may also find long journeys on strange forms of transport upsetting, so always consider the implications of any trip from his point of view.

Holidays are opportunities for all the family to be together, and no-one will be happier about that than your puppy.

GOING ON HOLIDAY

If like me, you enjoy exploring the countryside, you will find it even more fun with your puppy at your side. A well-organized trip with a well-behaved puppy is sure to be great fun for you and your family, but a lack of forward-planning combined with a poorly trained puppy is the perfect recipe for turning a dream holiday into a nightmare.

Holiday tips

The following are just a few of the factors that are worth considering before you go on holiday.
• Make sure that your puppy is fit and capable of doing the amount of exercise that you are planning to undertake (see pages 92–3).
• He must be fully vaccinated (see page 121).
• He should be responsive to basic training, especially to the re-call command (see page 82).
• Unless you are going camping – in which case you will only have to cope with the mess in your tent – your puppy should be fully toilet-trained (see pages 74–7).
• Organize your route, and decide where you are going to stop for rest, meal and toilet breaks.
• Reserve accommodation in a place that not only allows dogs, but actively encourages them and has appropriate facilities.
• Check in advance with the local tourist board that there are no restrictions on dogs in any of the areas that you are planning to visit. For instance, many beaches are closed to dogs during the summer.
• Decide in advance what you will do with your puppy when you cannot supervise him. If he has a puppy crate (see page 52), take it with you. Never leave him in the car in warm weather (see page 89).
• If it is possible, take sufficient provisions for your puppy to last the whole trip, as you may not be able to buy his normal brand of food while you are away. Suddenly

changing his food may upset his digestive system and cause a bout of diarrhoea, which is the last thing you will want on holiday.

• If your puppy is on any special medication, take adequate supplies.

• Ask at your vet centre for the names and telephone numbers of vet centres in the areas that you are planning to visit. Your vet may even have a colleague whom he or she can recommend you to contact in the event of an emergency.

• If you have not had your puppy permanently identified, now could be the time to do so (see page 101).

• Take plenty of old towels and bedding for your puppy in case he gets wet and cold.

• Pack your pooper-scoopers.

• If you are registered with a vehicle-breakdown service, make sure that it has the facilities for transporting dogs should you need its assistance.

• Make sure that your puppy has adequate third-party-liability insurance (see page 107).

MOVING HOUSE

If you are anything like most people, you will find moving house a very stressful event. Your puppy may not find it much fun either as, if he remains at home during the packing, you will probably have to keep him shut away to prevent him from straying through open doors. Some dogs will become very over-excited by all the activity in the house and may be difficult to control; others may become very anxious. No matter how your puppy reacts, he will certainly be confused, and will not understand why his territory is being systematically dismantled and removed by strangers.

Out of harm's way

If and when you move house, my advice would be to board your puppy with friends, relatives or at a good kennels (see pages 96–7), from just before the point at which you start to pack up your belongings right through until you are reasonably settled in your new house. In this way, your puppy will avoid all the hustle and bustle of the move itself, and you will be able to concentrate on the job in hand.

When you move house, boarding your puppy with friends or at his boarding kennels will keep him blissfully unaware of the bustle and stress that uprooting inevitably involves.

More importantly, you will also give yourself time to prepare the new house and garden for his arrival, as you will have to answer many of the same questions with which you were faced when you prepared to bring him home for the first time (see pages 50–2).

New house rules

You will have to create some new rules for your puppy. Where will he sleep? To which parts of the house will he have access? Which part of the garden will he be able to use as a toilet area? You will need to teach him where this is. Is the garden safe and secure?

When you bring your puppy home, help him to settle in. If he senses that you are happy in your new environment, he will feel more relaxed and should adjust to the strange surroundings without problems. The best thing about moving house is that, once you have all settled in, you can begin to explore with your puppy and to discover new walks and places to go.

Your puppy is missing

Do not say it could never happen to you: I have known plenty of people who have experienced losing their dog, and all of them thought that they were diligent-enough owners for it not to happen. Fortunately, many of them were reunited with their dogs sooner or later, but some were not.

If you think that your puppy has strayed off when out on a walk, or has somehow escaped from home, do not simply assume that he will be able to find his way back: you must act quickly to find him. The following is a checklist of the most important actions to take.

If your puppy seems to be lost on a walk

• He may have been distracted by a wild animal or another dog. Go to where you last saw him and keep shouting his name. Make as much noise as you can. It is very useful to train your puppy to a dog whistle so that, in situations such as this, you can re-call him

Scanning a lost dog who has a microchip implant under his skin will enable him to be quickly reunited with his owner.

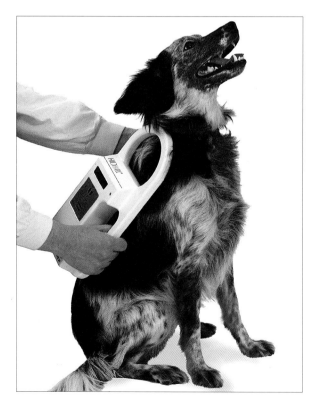

from places beyond the reach of your voice. Ask the instructor at your puppy playgroup (see page 80) or training class how to do this.
• Wave your arms so that you are more obvious from a distance. You may not be able to see your puppy but he may be able to see you, even if for some reason he cannot hear you.
• Only leave the place where you last saw your puppy when you are sure that he will not return to it. Retrace your steps to the starting point of the walk, dragging an article of your clothing on the ground as you do so. This will improve the chances of your puppy picking up your scent trail. Of course, he may already be back at the car or at home waiting for you!

If your puppy is definitely lost

• If you have a mobile telephone, call for the assistance of a few friends or family so that you can start a wider search for your puppy. Make sure that everyone who is involved is fully prepared and knows what he or she is doing before they start searching. If you are in a wild or unfamiliar place, you should consider calling on the advice of a local expert rescue organization.
• Notify every police station, animal-rescue centre, vet centre and boarding kennels in the area in which you last saw your puppy. Give them photographs and an accurate description of him.
• Contact the local-authority dog warden (if there is one in the area).
• If your puppy has been permanently identified (see opposite), notify the national register that he is missing (ask at your vet centre for details).
• Personally visit as many local houses as you can to ask whether anyone has seen your puppy.
• If he is insured against loss (see page 107), inform the company involved.
• Put up 'Missing' posters in the area in which you last saw your puppy, and in other public places such as shops, vet centres and pubs. Consider offering a reward: if your puppy is insured, the policy may cover the costs of advertising and/or rewards (see page 107).
• Visit the place where you last saw your puppy several times a day, especially at dawn and dusk.
• Regularly visit in person all the dog-rescue centres that you have already contacted.
• Finally, do not give up hope. Owners are sometimes reunited with their lost dogs many months after the dogs first went missing.

Identifying and registering your puppy

You are much more likely to be reunited with a lost puppy if you have permanently identified his body with a unique identity that is logged on to a national computer database (see below). You must also have a precise description of him: if your puppy is lost, you will want to tell as many people as possible exactly what he looks like, and if he is found you will need to prove that he is yours before taking him home.

Even if it is not a legal responsibility where you live, my advice is that, if at all possible, you should identify your puppy with either a tattoo or a microchip implant. In places where tattoo and microchip schemes are in operation, these should be looked for whenever a lost or stray dog is found.

Ask at your vet centre for details and costs relating to all the identification and registration schemes in use where you live.

Marking with a tattoo • A tattoo is normally marked on the inside of a dog's ear flap, or on his inner thigh. It is not a painful procedure, and requires no special equipment to read it. However, the disadvantages of a tattoo are that it may fade with age and, on an ear flap, may become distorted by growth or injury. Some owners may also consider tattoos to be unsightly.

Implanting a microchip • A microchip is a very small device that is injected under a dog's skin, usually in his neck. The microchip does not send out a constant signal, but requires an electronic scanner to 'read' the identity with which it is programmed. The advantage of a microchip is that it should be permanent; the disadvantage is that it is not possible to tell, just by looking at a dog, whether he has one. There is also no guarantee that a person who finds him will be aware of such a device.

A microchip is very tiny and is injected under a dog's skin through a needle. The procedure is quick and no more uncomfortable to most dogs than a vaccination.

RESPONSIBLE DOG-OWNERSHIP

The precise laws relating to dog-ownership may vary depending on where you live, but you can assume that, as a new dog-owner, you will have to obey some national laws and other more local ones. In general, these laws aim to protect the welfare of all dogs, and to ensure that they are not a public nuisance. Any and all legal responsibilities apply to the person in charge of a dog, not just to his owner. Should an offence be committed, the relevant person may be prosecuted and, if he or she is found guilty, penalties such as fines and even prison sentences may apply. You should find out what your new legal responsibilities regarding your puppy will be, by asking at your local police station or citizens'-advice centre.

As a brief guide to your legal responsibilities as a dog-owner, below are some of the major and most relevant points covered by the laws relating to dogs that are currently in force in England and Wales.

• In public places, a dog must wear a collar with the name and address of his owner either permanently written on the collar itself or engraved on a disk or other badge attached to the collar.

• It is an offence to be cruel to a dog in any way. This means harming a dog either physically or mentally, including beating, kicking or terrifying him, carrying or transporting him in any way that causes him suffering and failing to seek medical attention for him when necessary. It does not matter whether the cruelty is intended or not: ignorance is no excuse.

• It is an offence to abandon a dog – temporarily or permanently – without reasonable cause. This includes letting a dog free to fend for himself as a stray, or keeping him shut away without care and attention.

• If a dog worries livestock on agricultural land, the person in charge of the dog at the time may be liable to prosecution by the owner of that land.

• The keeper of a dog may be liable for any damage caused by that dog to another person's property.

• It may be an offence for a person in charge of a dog to fail to remove faeces deposited by the dog in designated areas, such as on footpaths, grass verges or beaches, or in parks, recreation areas or gutters.

Health and hygiene

Keeping your puppy healthy does not simply mean taking him to the vet when he is unwell. You will need to implement a range of healthcare measures at home, including routine health-checks, grooming and parasite control. You must also take him to your vet centre for regular development checks and vaccinations.

Vet centres

If your puppy is injured or becomes ill, you will want the best medical attention available for him. It is comforting to know that veterinary services are available 24 hours a day, 365 days a year from most vet centres. Even those that do not provide out-of-hours services themselves should make sure that the needs of their patients are catered for in emergencies.

There are likely to be a number of vet centres in your area, and you should spend the time and effort required to choose the one that will best suit you and your puppy (see pages 106–7). Do not wait until there is something wrong with him, but make your choice and register before you even obtain your puppy. Remember that you will need to take him for his first health-check as soon as you collect him (see page 71).

The vast majority of vet centres are run as private businesses, so remember that you will have to pay for most of the services that you use. Health insurance is now an option for dog-owners, and I would strongly advise you to think about taking this out for your puppy (see page 107).

VETERINARY STAFF

The staff at your vet centre will be a mine of useful information about puppy care, and will give you plenty of useful hints and tips to help you plan for your puppy's arrival. They will not only treat him when he is unwell, but should also provide a range of preventive-medicine services, including parasite control, vaccination, dental care and dietary advice.

There are a number of people who play a part in the day-to-day running of a large vet centre, including receptionists, animal-care assistants and even a centre manager, but those people with whom you will have the most contact are the vets and veterinary nurses.

Veterinary surgeons (Vets)

It takes the same, or better, school qualifications and a similar length of university training to become a vet as it does to become a doctor. Although many vets eventually become specialists in the care of just one or two types of animal (such as dogs and cats), every vet is qualified to treat all creatures – great and small.

The vet who looks after your puppy will not only be his physician, but much more besides, including his surgeon, dentist, anaesthetist and psychiatrist!

receptionist   animal-care assistant   trainee veterinary nurse   vet (associate)

As part of their training, veterinary students must spend time gaining experience in vet centres, and will carry out some procedures under supervision.

Many of the tasks that were previously undertaken by vets are now being made the responsibility of the veterinary nurses at some centres, to give the vets time to concentrate on more specialist work. Some vets will go on to take further qualifications in specific areas of veterinary care, such as dermatology or orthopaedics.

Veterinary nurses

Veterinary nurses are skilled, dedicated and highly trained individuals who are, in my experience, the backbone of many vet centres.

Just a few of their many responsibilities are to run the operating theatre, to assist vets with surgical and medical procedures, to look after in-patients, to run the drugs dispensary, to carry out laboratory tests and to help in organizing special clinics such as puppy playgroups (see page 80). Veterinary nurses may also carry out some medical treatments and minor surgical procedures on their own.

A good vet centre (right) will invest considerable sums of money in employing and training knowledgeable, skilled and caring staff (below), all of whom will be dedicated to providing you and your puppy with the best of care.

vet (centre owner)   head veterinary nurse   veterinary nurse   centre manager

The layout of a typical vet centre

| What the client sees | Behind the scenes | Work surfaces |

TYPES OF VET CENTRE

There are several different types of vet centre. Some have the facilities and staff to treat animals of any sort – large or small – including horses, farm stock, dogs, cats and other pet animals. Others concentrate solely on the care of domestic pets, including some of the more exotic types of animal such as reptiles.

The largest and best-equipped centres may be called veterinary hospitals, and usually have staff living on the premises. The smallest centres are often simple clinics without surgical, diagnostic or in-patient facilities of their own, and may be part of a group of centres. Between these extremes are centres of all sizes.

More and more centres now run open days in order to allow current and prospective clients to see behind the scenes. To give you an idea of what to expect when you visit a vet centre, above is the plan of a typical centre with facilities for both dog and cat patients.

Veterinary services

The type, nature and range of services available from a particular vet centre will depend on the interests and the expertise of the people who run it. Some centres offer a full range of services aimed at pet-owners; others are more specialized. For instance, a centre may concentrate solely on skin diseases, and may only take on cases referred to them by other vets.

The kind of vet centre that will be most useful to you should offer the types of services described here.

Accident-and-emergency care

If you need any veterinary help out of hours, you will normally have to telephone your vet centre. Remember that, after normal working hours, the vet or nurse to whom you speak may be unfamiliar to you. Equally, he or she may not know your puppy personally, and may not have his records immediately at hand. Let the vet or the nurse lead the conversation. Answer his or her questions accurately, and listen carefully to any instructions. It is a good idea to write them down.

The vet may wish to see your puppy. Although a home visit may be essential in some cases, if possible and appropriate the vet will request that you take your puppy to the vet centre. With better facilities there

A normal consultation will last about 15 minutes and will be conducted by your vet; routine health-checks and procedures may be carried out by a qualified veterinary nurse.

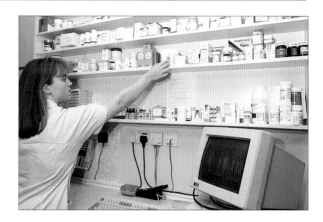

The vast majority of vet centres run their own in-house drugs dispensaries. These are used to supply medicines directly to animal-owners, as prescribed by the vets.

than are available in the back of the car, he or she will be able to examine and treat him more effectively.

It is worth remembering that – in many cases – the vet on duty at night will also have worked all day and may work all the next day before he or she has any time off. Be sensible about how you use the out-of-hours services available from your vet centre, and try not to abuse them. You should also expect to pay a small fee supplement for these services.

Consultations

During working hours, your vet centre should offer you the option of an individual consultation with your vet for him or her to examine your puppy or to discuss any other health-related matter. 'Open' surgeries are run on a first-come, first-seen basis, but most centres also offer fixed appointments.

The length of a consultation will vary, but it should last for at least 15 minutes. In my view, a vet cannot examine a dog, question his owner, make a diagnosis and decide on a treatment in less time than this. Expect to pay a fixed fee for the appointment, plus extra for any tests, drugs or other products used.

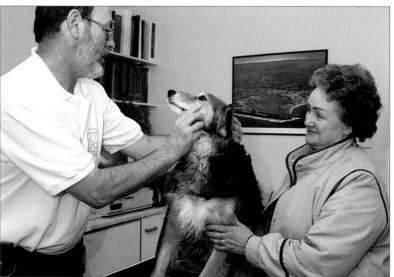

Diagnostics

If your puppy is off-colour, your vet may wish to carry out some diagnostic tests to try to establish what is causing the problem. The tests may include relatively straightforward procedures, including the use of a stethoscope, a thermometer or an ophthalmoscope (an instrument used to look in detail at a dog's eyes), and may be carried out while you are present.

More complex diagnostic procedures, such as blood tests, radiology (taking X-ray pictures), the recording of an ECG (ElectroCardioGram: used to measure the electrical activity in a dog's heart), endoscopy (looking into body cavities using a long, thin, flexible camera) or an ultrasound scan may also be necessary, and for these you will probably have to book your puppy into your vet centre as an in-patient.

Drugs dispensary

In the vast majority of cases that require therapy using drugs, treatment will start at your vet centre, but you will be expected to continue the administration of the drugs at home. Almost all vet centres run their own dispensaries to supply these drugs.

Surgery

Neutering, dental descaling and polishing, removing a growth or a broken nail, repairing a skin wound and mending a fractured bone are all considered surgical procedures. All vet centres (apart from the smallest clinic-only centres) should have full surgical facilities, including general-anaesthetic equipment, a sterile operating theatre stocked with appropriate surgical instruments, and a post-anaesthetic recovery area. The facilities in the most advanced vet centres are very similar to those available in human hospitals.

It is now possible to implant artificial hip joints in dogs and to carry out heart surgery, but the complexity of surgery undertaken at a particular vet centre will depend upon the level of equipment and the expertise of the staff at that centre.

Services for healthy dogs

Remember that your vet centre is not just there for when things go wrong: it should also offer you a range of other products and services that will help to keep your puppy healthy.

Almost all centres will be able to vaccinate puppies and adult dogs (see pages 120–1), and should stock a range of healthcare products, including those needed for dental care (see pages 114–15) and parasite control

THE COSTS OF VETERINARY CARE

If your puppy needs surgery of any kind, you must expect a reasonably large but realistic bill. Remember that the technical skill required by a surgeon is just the same whether the operation is on a human or a dog, and that the facilities in the best vet centres are similar to those available in human hospitals.

Indeed, much of the surgical and anaesthetic equipment now used by vets was developed to treat humans, and has been adapted for use on animals.

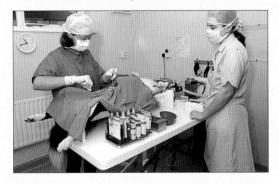

(see pages 116–19). A selection of special diets and food items, formulated to help in treating certain conditions, is also available from many vet centres.

Obtaining such products is, however, only part of ensuring good healthcare for your puppy. Almost more important is the advice you will need in order to select the most appropriate products and to use them properly. A number of vet centres now employ veterinary nurses who are specially trained to advise clients on all aspects of dog healthcare, including nutrition and behaviour. The nurses may offer advice on a one-to-one basis, but may run group clinics as well. Puppy playgroups (see page 80) and 'weight-watchers' sessions are now commonplace.

Referrals

Very few vet centres have all the necessary equipment and expertise to be able to provide every client with every healthcare service that their pets may require during their lives. If your puppy at some stage needs treatment that is not available at your centre, your vet may suggest that you take him to another centre.

If it is necessary, your vet should also be able to refer your puppy to another professional involved in animal care, such as a dog-behaviour expert or even a physiotherapist.

Choosing a vet centre

Research shows that most dog-owners simply use the vet centre that happens to be nearest to their homes, but, as you will have learned on the previous pages, not all vet centres are the same. The centre that is geographically most convenient may well turn out to be the one best-suited to your needs, but do not assume that this will be the case. Ideally, you should make your decision well before you even collect your puppy, so that you can benefit from all the advice available as you prepare to become a dog-owner.

Investigate the alternatives for vet centres, if any exist, by following the steps below. Take your time with this research: it will pay off in the long term.

1 Look in your local telephone directory for names and addresses, and make a list of all the vet centres within 20 to 30 minutes' drive. This is the furthest that you should need to travel in an emergency.

2 Create a shortlist of those centres with the facilities and expertise to treat dogs.

3 Make a quick, unannounced visit to all the vet centres on your shortlist and, while you are there, take note of the following aspects.
• The difficulty of the journey.
• The ease of access to the premises.
• The state of repair of the premises.
• The cleanliness of the waiting room.
• The appearance and attitude of the reception staff.

Ask for information about the centre, including details of all the services available, background on the staff, the centre's opening times and the kinds of fees charged. Find out whether it would be possible to arrange a tour of the centre. If not, do not consider that centre further. Before you leave, wait around looking at the noticeboard for long enough to discover how clients are handled at reception and on the telephone.

4 Speak to any dog-owning friends to obtain their opinions of the centres on your initial list. Then, armed with the information on each centre and with your friends' views in mind, prepare a new shortlist.

5 Arrange to view behind the scenes at the centres you have shortlisted. If possible, go as a family or take a friend, as second opinions are always valuable. While you are there, try to meet some of the veterinary staff. On your visit, take note of the following aspects.
• The overall cleanliness and state of repair.
• The appearance, friendliness and professionalism of the veterinary staff.

Finally, go home, think about everything that you have seen and heard, and then make your decision.

Changing your vet

You may need to change your vet if you move house, and, if so, you should select a new vet centre in the same way as before. When you register at the new centre, the receptionist will contact your old centre to obtain all your puppy's medical records. You may also consider moving to a new centre if you become unhappy with the service that you are receiving, but do talk through any grievance with the staff. The problem may well have occurred because of a breakdown in communications, and it would be a pity to leave a good centre over a simple misunderstanding.

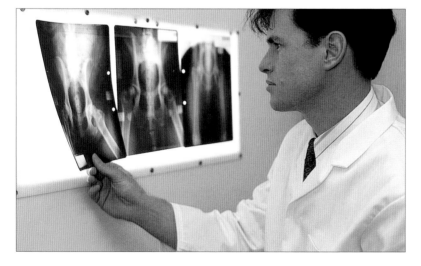

Having completed their training, many vets specialize in particular areas of veterinary science, such as radiology or orthopaedics. Your own vet will refer your puppy to an appropriate expert, should the need arise.

GETTING A SECOND OPINION

If your puppy is unwell and his condition does not seem to be improving despite treatment, your vet may suggest that he is examined by another vet for a second opinion. He or she may suggest a more specialist vet from the same centre, or someone working elsewhere. If you need to take your puppy to another centre, your vet should make all the necessary arrangements for you. At any time, you may arrange a second opinion from another vet independently, although some specialists will only take cases referred to them by other vets.

Putting your puppy at ease

It is not surprising that many dogs actively dislike visting their vet centre: many only go there when they are ill or injured, and then they are prodded, poked and often injected. No matter how kind or considerate your vet and veterinary nurses are, your puppy may not thank them for some of the things that they will do to him. However, by taking him to the centre for his regular health-checks, the good experiences should outnumber the not-so-good ones. Take him with you whenever you go to the centre – even if only to pay a bill – and make sure that he has a good time. The nurses will not need any excuses to play with him!

HEALTH INSURANCE

You can work out the yearly cost of some healthcare procedures for your puppy, but it is impossible to predict the cost of any veterinary care that he may require if he is ill or suffers an injury. There may also be no way of telling how sophisticated the treatment will be, or for how long your puppy will need it.

Fortunately, it is now possible to insure against the costs of treatment, and, for an annual premium, most insurance policies will guarantee to pay all veterinary fees up to a maximum amount in each year. When choosing a policy, be sure to read the small print and, if in any doubt, consult an insurance advisor. Annual premiums will vary, but if you own a large breed of dog you may have to pay a supplement.

I would wholeheartedly recommend that you take out health insurance for your puppy. Believe me, there is nothing worse than seeing an owner – distraught about his or her dog's illness or injury – having to cope with the additional worry of how to pay for his care. Your vet centre is run as a business, and you cannot expect your vet to reduce the fees or to give you credit because you do not have sufficient available funds.

A typical policy may cover the following aspects.
• Veterinary fees for every illness and accident, including physiotherapy, acupuncture, herbal and homoeopathic medicines, hospitalization and referral.
• Death following illness: the cost of your puppy will be reimbursed.
• Death following an accident: the cost of your puppy will be reimbursed.
• Loss by theft or straying: the cost of your puppy will be reimbursed.
• Boarding-kennel fees for your puppy if you are taken into hospital for more than four days.
• Holiday-cancellation costs if your puppy has emergency surgery up to seven days before you go on holiday, or goes missing while you are away.
• Advertising and reward costs should your puppy become lost or be stolen.
• Third-party liability in case your puppy causes damage or injury and you are legally liable.
• A 'burglar reward' if your puppy catches an intruder who has broken into your home.

Unexpected veterinary fees can be an unwelcome burden. The chart below indicates the relative costs incurred in the first year of owning a puppy who suffers a serious illness.

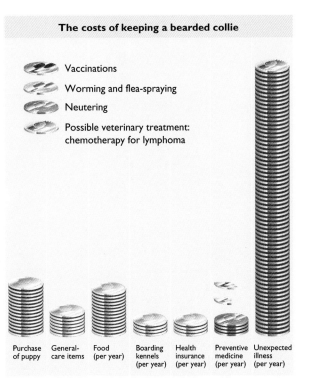

The costs of keeping a bearded collie

Vaccinations

Worming and flea-spraying

Neutering

Possible veterinary treatment: chemotherapy for lymphoma

Purchase of puppy | General-care items | Food (per year) | Boarding kennels (per year) | Health insurance (per year) | Preventive medicine (per year) | Unexpected illness (per year)

Health-monitoring

You are an essential part of your puppy's healthcare team. As his owner, it is you who have ultimate responsibility for his diet, his exercise and his day-to-day care. Your puppy will also rely on you to identify when he is unwell, and to seek veterinary attention for him when necessary.

CARRYING OUT HEALTH-CHECKS

Unfortunately, the signs and symptoms of many conditions may not be as obvious as those associated with a broken leg or a skin cut, so you should carry out a simple health-check on your puppy at least once a week. By examining him thoroughly on this regular basis, you are much more likely to pick up any health problems before they become crises.

These health-checks will also quickly familiarize your puppy with the experience of being restrained and examined. As he grows up, he will therefore see them as routine and very normal events in his life.

When? • This is obviously up to you, but you should try to arrange that your puppy's good behaviour during his health-checks will be rewarded by something more interesting than being put to bed for the night. You should weigh your puppy at the same time of day on each occasion, as natural variations in his body weight that will occur during a 24-hour period may be misleading. A good time to carry out a health-check on your puppy is when you are grooming him (see pages 110–13).

Where ? • You will find it much easier to restrain and examine your puppy if he is off the floor and on a table (this should have a non-slip surface).

Who? • Ideally, all the members of your family should become experienced at carrying out health-checks on your puppy. If he becomes fully accustomed to different people examining him, he will be much better-behaved when he is restrained and checked over by a stranger, such as your vet.

A basic health-check

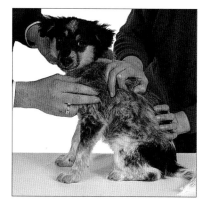

Hair and skin

Check for the following problems.
• Greasy hair, hair loss or dandruff.
• Red, inflamed areas of skin.
• An abnormal smell to the coat.
• Evidence of fleas (see page 119).
• Areas of skin scaling or crusting.
• Lumps and bumps.
• Foreign bodies (such as thorns).
• Mats in the fur (see page 111).

Eyes

Check for the following problems.
• Tear-stained fur around the eyes.
• Reddened inner eyelids.
• The appearance of the third eyelids at the corners of the eyes.
• Cloudiness within the eyeball.
• Squinting.
• Dull surfaces to the eyes.
• Foreign bodies.

Ears

Check for the following problems.
• Discharge or debris at one or both of the ear holes.
• Red, inflamed ear holes or inner sides of the ear flaps.
• A noticeable, abnormal smell at the ear holes.
• Any unusual swelling of the ear flaps.

What does a health-check involve?

There are certain important examinations that should be a part of your health-check routine, although the order in which you carry them out is unimportant. Listed below are just some of the symptoms that could indicate potential medical problems.

There is sure to be one question that keeps cropping up while you are examining your puppy: 'Is this normal?' Each dog is an individual, and what could at first sight appear to be an anatomical abnormality on your puppy may just be a normal variation. For instance, you may be concerned if you notice a large black spot on his otherwise pink tongue, but many dogs' tongues have irregular black markings on them. A chow chow's entire tongue is usually black.

The more you examine your puppy, the better you will get to know his anatomical characteristics, and the easier you will find it to recognize abnormalities. Use your eyes, your fingers and your nose to identify anything unusual in the way your puppy looks, feels or smells. Watch how he reacts to being handled: any

unusual resentment to being examined could indicate that you have touched on something painful. If you are ever in any doubt, seek veterinary attention.

You should also pay close attention to the nature of your puppy's body waste, so that you will know if this changes in any way. Through living with your puppy, you will learn what is normal behaviour for him, and should notice immediately if something is wrong.

WEIGHING YOUR PUPPY

If your puppy is no larger than a cat, you should be able to weigh him on a set of bathroom scales in his carrying basket. If he is any bigger than this, you will have to pick him up to weigh him. If he is too heavy for you to lift up comfortably, you may need to weigh him at your vet centre: most centres now have electronic weigh platforms especially for this purpose.

Mouth

Check for the following problems.
• Inflamed gums (see page 114).
• Broken teeth.
• Brown staining of the teeth, especially near the gums.
• Unusually bad breath.
• Reddened, inflamed skin near the lips.
• Foreign bodies.

Feet

Check for the following problems.
• Overlong nails (especially the dew claws).
• Cracked or frayed nails.
• Cracked or damaged pads.
• Red, inflamed skin between the toes or pads.
• Fur mats between the toes.
• Foreign bodies.

Grooming your puppy

Your puppy's skin is his largest body organ, and at birth accounts for nearly a quarter of his weight. Strong but stretchy, it wraps and protects his skeleton, muscles and most other vital body structures, and allows him to experience touch, pressure, itchiness, pain, heat and cold. It also stores water, vitamins, fats, carbohydrates and proteins. The most obvious role of your puppy's skin, however, is that it produces his hair-coat, his nails and his foot pads.

Skin disorders are among the most common of all canine medical problems. By grooming your puppy regularly and frequently, feeding him a high-quality, balanced diet and preventing infestations of common skin parasites such as fleas (see pages 118–19), you will help to ensure that his coat remains in top condition.

WHAT IS HAIR?

Hair is dead. It is mostly protein, and is produced by special structures called follicles within the skin. A dog's diet has a profound effect on the quantity and quality of his hair: inadequate nutrition may lead to a poor, brittle, dry or thin hair-coat.

Types of coat

There are several different types of hair-coat in dogs.

'Normal' coat • This type of coat – such as that of a German shepherd – is made up of long, bristly 'guard' hairs and many shorter undercoat hairs.

Short coat • This coat may be either coarse or fine. A rottweiler has a coarse coat containing many guard hairs, and a less dense undercoat. Breeds with a fine, short coat include the boxer and the dachshund; this coat is the most dense of all.

Long coat • This may be fine in texture, as in the cocker spaniel, or woolly, as in the poodle.

Coat colours • The many different coat colours are combinations of just two pigments: a black/brown pigment and a red/yellow one.

Hair fact file

• The hair lies in different directions, called hair tracts, on different parts of a dog's body. Generally, it slopes backwards along the body and downwards towards the feet. This is thought to reduce 'drag'

Grooming a long-haired puppy

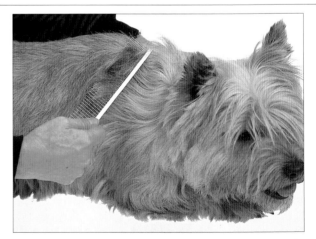

1 After checking for fur mats (see opposite), use a slicker brush (as shown) or a pin brush to remove loose hairs and any debris trapped in the coat. Use the brush gently but firmly, reaching right down to the depths of the coat. Begin with the least-sensitive areas of your puppy's body, and leave his head until last.

2 Repeat the whole process using a comb. This will help to remove any hairs loosened by brushing, and will ensure that no tangles remain. Finish off by gently wiping away any dirt or discharge from the hair around your puppy's eyes, and from the undersides of his ear flaps, using moist face-wipes.

when the dog moves, and to encourage water to run off his body without soaking through to the skin.

• Hair grows in cycles. A hair grows until it reaches a length governed by a dog's genes, and then, after a variable period (depending on factors such as ambient temperature and daylight length), the hair is shed.

• A dog does not go bald when shedding his coat, or moulting, because no two hairs near each other are at the same part of the growth cycle at the same time.

• Most dogs moult once in spring, when they grow a coarse, thin coat, and again in autumn, when they grow a thicker winter coat. Some dogs, kept in artificial lighting and heating, may moult all year round.

• Hair grows at different rates on different parts of the body. In some places on some dogs it can grow over 5 mm (¼ in) per week. Having been shaved, a short coat may take six months to regrow, but a fine, long coat may take 18 months to do so.

Why groom your puppy?

A tangled, matted or dirty coat does not insulate a dog's body effectively, and fails to protect the underlying skin from damage. Without adequate grooming, both the hair-coat and the skin that produces it are vulnerable to disease.

In the wild, a wolf has to look after his own coat, and will use his tongue as a flannel and his teeth as a comb. Many pet dogs look more glamorous than their wild relatives because they have unnatural but 'fashionable' coats created through selective breeding. Unfortunately, some of the more unusual kinds of hair-coat seem prone to matting, and so can be very difficult for dogs to look after by themselves.

When to groom

Some dogs really enjoy being groomed, but many adult dogs who have not been accustomed to regular grooming from puppyhood often resent it. As soon as your puppy has settled in with you, start a daily grooming routine. At first, just groom him on his back for a few minutes, and reward him for staying calm. Gradually increase the grooming to include the more sensitive parts of his body, such as under his tail and between his hindlegs.

The time that you will need to spend on grooming will depend on your puppy's coat type, but, ideally, you should groom him thoroughly once a week. You can carry out routine health-checks (see pages 108–9) at the same time. Puppies who are moulting their woolly juvenile coats need more frequent grooming.

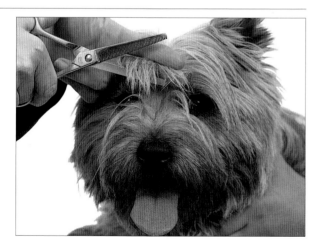

3 If your puppy has an overlong fringe, trim it using a special pair of thinning scissors. Comb the fringe forwards towards his nose, then cut about halfway down the length of the fringe. Comb again, and repeat the thinning if the fringe is still too long. Be sure to protect your puppy's eyes when using scissors.

REMOVING A FUR MAT

A mat usually forms from loose hairs that have become tangled. If you find a mat, do not try to 'snatch' a brush or comb through it: you will not clear the mat and you will hurt your puppy. To remove it you will need a tool called a mat-breaker. Hold the base of the mat with the fingers of one hand, and the mat-breaker in the other. Work at the mat from the edge and it will gradually come apart. When you have cleared it, brush through the remaining hair with a slicker brush.

Where to groom

Always groom your puppy in the same place so that he becomes accustomed to the routine. If possible, you should groom him on a table covered with a non-slip mat, as you will find it much easier to control him if he is off the floor and on unusual territory. Vets and professional dog-groomers do not just use tables to be kind to their own backs!

Who should do the grooming?

Try not to think of grooming your puppy as a chore. It will be an excellent way of bonding with him, as well as practising essential handling skills, so ideally all the members of your family should be involved.

What equipment do you need?

You will need a brush, a comb and some human face-wipes. The range of grooming equipment now available is enormous, so my advice would be to ask a professional dog-groomer to recommend tools that he or she feels are best-suited to your puppy's coat.

Cutting your puppy's nails

You should regularly check the length of your puppy's nails. When you are at your vet centre, ask your vet or a veterinary nurse to show you their ideal length. Never attempt to cut your puppy's nails without first having watched a demonstration by the vet or nurse.

BATHING YOUR PUPPY

Some owners bath their dogs regularly, but rarely do healthy dogs smell bad enough to need the kind of excessive bathing that they may receive. In my experience, dogs who smell usually have unhealthy skin that needs medical attention. Dogs with very greasy or dry skin may also have a problem that requires specific treatment.

I would recommend that you only bath your puppy when it is absolutely necessary, as frequent bathing using shampoos may damage the water-resistant qualities of his coat.

A rinse with a hosepipe may be all that is needed if your puppy is just muddy. If he really is filthy and

Grooming a short-haired puppy

1 Using a rubber-fingered glove, rub your puppy's coat in all directions to remove loose hairs. You will be amazed at how much hair is dragged away by the rubber knobs on the glove.

2 Having worked your way over the puppy's whole body with the glove, use a soft brush to give the coat a good sheen. Finally, wipe away any discharge around the eyes and ear flaps, using moist face-wipes.

has rolled in something that you would rather he hadn't, make sure if you decide to bath him that you use a shampoo that is pH-balanced to a normal dog's skin (the range is 5.5 to 7.5) for his body, and a 'no-tears' baby shampoo for his face. A dog with a long coat will benefit from the use of a suitable conditioner: ask your vet or a veterinary nurse, or a professional dog-groomer, for advice on this.

I would suggest that you bath your puppy outside, using a hose-pipe. If you prefer, however, and you are not too worried about your bathroom looking like the inside of a washing machine after a long rinse cycle, then you can bath your puppy there instead!

Bath-time may be a source of some amusement for the people involved, but it is important that your puppy does not see it as a game or you may find it difficult to keep control of him.

You will need

- A non-slip mat for the bottom of the bath.
- An apron for yourself.
- Shampoo (and conditioner, if appropriate).
- Plenty of towels.
- Cotton-wool plugs for your puppy's ears (ask a professional groomer how to insert these, and do not forget to remove them afterwards).
- A human helper.
- Your well-brushed puppy, wearing his collar (the helper will need to hold on to this, to prevent your puppy from trying to escape at a critical moment). Beware, however, as the dye used in some coloured collars may run and you may inadvertently end up giving your puppy a blue rinse!

What to do

1 The first thing to do is to close the bathroom door. Do you want a soapy puppy running riot around your house? Dilute the shampoo before you start, or it may take a long time to rinse out. When both you and your helper are ready, carefully lift your puppy into the bath. If he is well-behaved and calm, reward him. If he seems anxious, just be calm yourself and get on with it. Do not attempt to reassure him, or you will simply confirm his worst fears.

2 Test the water temperature, then wet your puppy's coat using a shower attachment or a jug: start at his feet and then work up his body, finally soaking his

back. Shampoo and thoroughly wash his body, then gently wet his head and wash it with baby shampoo before rinsing him off thoroughly. If you are using a conditioner, follow the instructions on the bottle.

3 Towel-dry your puppy while he is still in the bath, then take him somewhere appropriate to finish him off with a hairdryer. This is a strange experience for most puppies, but one to which they will quickly become accustomed. While using the hairdryer, brush through your puppy's coat, keeping your hand in the airflow. You will then know instantly if you are getting too close. Do not blow-dry your puppy's face. When he is dry, comb him off and admire your handiwork.

GETTING EXPERT HELP

If your puppy has an unusual coat that requires special care, or you find him difficult to groom properly, seek specific coat-care advice from a suitably qualified dog-groomer. If your puppy starts scratching excessively, or his skin or coat looks abnormal in any way (see page 108), do not hesitate to take him along to your vet centre for a check-up. Skin conditions that may seem trivial at first can very rapidly become serious.

Dental care

By far the most common oral disease of dogs affects the gums and supporting structures of the teeth. It occurs as a result of the build-up of bacterial plaque on the teeth, and is called periodontal disease (see below).

It may take months or even years for serious disease to develop, but the problems start while a dog is still a young puppy. In the early stages this condition is reversible, so routine dental care for puppies is vital.

Teeth fact file

- Like humans, dogs are not born with teeth.
- The teeth are living structures that contain blood vessels and nerves, and so respond to pain.
- A puppy's first set of milk, or deciduous, teeth begins to erupt when he is between three and five weeks old (see pages 26–30). In all, the puppy will have 28 milk teeth.
- When a puppy is about three months old, his milk teeth will be replaced by his adult or permanent ones. These teeth (42 in all) should have erupted by the time the puppy is seven months old.
- Adult dogs have four different types of teeth, called incisors, canines, premolars and molars.

Incisors • These are the small front teeth used for cutting, nibbling, grooming and biting. In most dogs, the incisors in the upper jaw should come down just in front of those on the lower jaw.

Canines • These are the large and very obvious 'eye-teeth', used for holding and tearing food. They are also important in keeping a dog's tongue in his mouth and holding his lips in position.

Premolars • These lie behind the canine teeth, and are used for shearing, cutting and holding food.

Molars • These are at the back of the mouth, and have flattened surfaces for grinding and chewing food.

PERIODONTAL DISEASE

The outer surfaces of a dog's teeth are made of enamel, the hardest material in his body. On a daily basis his teeth become covered in bacterial plaque, but, through chewing, this plaque is to some extent wiped away from the smooth enamel. How much remains may depend to some extent on the dog's diet: for example, some moist foods tend to stick to the teeth and so may exacerbate the build-up of plaque.

Plaque is soft, but rapidly hardens to produce a substance called calculus or tartar which gradually thickens over time and has an outer covering of more plaque. Unlike enamel, calculus is rough and so plaque is more difficult to remove from it. Bacteria near the gum edges irritate the gum and cause it to become red and swell – a condition called gingivitis – and, as the gum grows more inflamed, other damaging bacteria become involved. The gum may then begin to recede around a tooth, which will eventually work loose.

The key to preventing periodontal disease is the regular removal of plaque before its presence can cause damage to the edges of the gums. This can be achieved in the following ways.

Daily tooth-brushing

Regular and frequent brushing using a special dog toothbrush and toothpaste is a very effective way of removing bacterial plaque from your puppy's teeth.

Despite the fact that he will lose all his milk teeth within six months, you should start brushing your puppy's teeth as soon as you bring him home. As with so many procedures, the sooner he and you become used to tooth-brushing, the better.

1 At first, accustom your puppy to the feel of the brush by holding his mouth closed and placing the brush in the pouch formed by his cheek for several seconds. Reward him with a rawhide chew for staying calm. Each day, keep the brush in his mouth for a little longer, and begin to move it about.

Without the benefit of tooth-brushing, many dogs suffer from a build-up of calculus on their teeth. This is associated with severe periodontal disease, and may be painful.

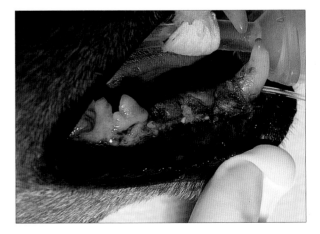

2 When your puppy is used to this experience, start brushing the outsides of his back teeth. First dip the brush in water, then hold it at 45 degrees to the teeth and move it in small circles.

3 The gums at the front of a dog's mouth seem more sensitive, so only move on to these once your puppy is more familiar with tooth-brushing. (Brushing the insides of his teeth is much less important, as his tongue will make a good job of keeping these surfaces clean.)

4 Once your puppy is accustomed to having his teeth brushed with water, ask your vet or a veterinary nurse to recommend a suitable toothpaste for use on his teeth.

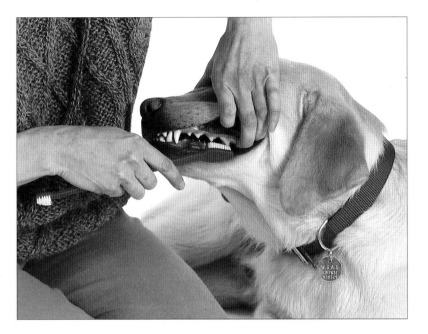

Diet

The effects of different kinds of diet – such as dry and moist foods (see page 59) – on the development of periodontal disease are still a matter of debate, but it may help to remove plaque if you offer your puppy large pieces of raw vegetables and tough, fibrous meat such as heart, ox skirt, cheek muscle or bovine trachea to chew on once a week. However, do not overdo this or you may upset the overall balance of his diet.

Chewing on bones devoid of meat will do little more than wear down the surfaces of your puppy's teeth, and may even break them. In my view, such bones have no place in preventing periodontal disease.

Special toothbrushes are available for puppies and small breeds. As your puppy grows, you may need to change his brush. Adult-dog toothbrushes are available (as shown), but just as good is a human brush with medium/firm bristles.

Visiting the dentist

Your dental-care efforts at home are no guarantee that your puppy will not need special dental care from time to time. Tooth-brushing will not remove calculus, and, if this forms, it will need removing using an ultrasonic descaler. This procedure is carried out under a general anaesthetic. You should ask your vet to carry out a thorough dental check-up on your puppy once a year.

TOYS AND CHEWS

Special toys intended for dogs to chew on are claimed by their manufacturers to be effective aids in the control of periodontal disease. One type has grooves in it, designed to be filled with small amounts of toothpaste: when a dog chews on the toy, the grooves squeeze the toothpaste over his teeth. There are also nylon toys made in many shapes and sizes, including balls, Frisbees and bones, all of which are claimed to be useful supplements but are not alternatives to regular tooth-brushing. If you decide to buy any dental chew for your puppy, make absolutely sure that it is suitable for his size and temperament. Offering him a 'rawhide' chew once or twice a week may also help.

Parasite prevention

Parasites are organisms that live in or on animals and derive their nourishment from them. Like humans – as well as most other mammals, birds, fish and reptiles – dogs are covered with and also contain numerous parasites: in fact, they are walking zoos!

The best-known of the parasites that live in dogs are tapeworms and roundworms, while fleas are their most common external parasite in many countries (see pages 118–19). Worms and fleas can cause disease, so you should regularly treat your puppy for them, even if you do not think that there are any in or on him. You should also take action to control fleas in your house.

TAPEWORMS

Perhaps the most common tapeworm to affect dogs in the UK is called *Dipylidium caninum*. Adult tapeworms of this type live in a dog's small intestine. They consist of many segments, and may grow 50 cm (20 in) long.

How does a dog become infested?

Individual segments of an adult tapeworm, containing eggs, break off inside a dog's intestines. They find their way to the outside world through his anus and release their eggs. A flea larva (or a louse) in the environment may eat some of these eggs, which will then continue their development inside its body.

As an adult, the flea will search for an animal to jump aboard to suck blood. This may be the same dog, another dog, a cat or even a person. The flea may irritate the skin, causing the animal to nibble at this area. He may swallow the flea, which will release immature tapeworms into his intestines – and so the cycle continues.

What are the signs of infestation?

There may be no visible signs if there are only a few tapeworms inside a dog's intestines. However, sometimes segments may be seen wriggling on the fur around the anus, or on the ground. Very heavy infestations may cause obvious anal irritation and digestive upsets.

Are puppies vulnerable?

Yes. If there are fleas in their environments carrying immature tapeworms, puppies may be infested. It takes three weeks from the time a flea is swallowed until the adult tapeworm produces more eggs, so the earliest that you would see any signs in your puppy are when he has been with you for a few weeks (unless he came to you infested). The younger the puppy, the more serious a tapeworm infestation is likely to be.

Can people be infested?

Yes. While playing with a dog, a child or an adult may accidentally swallow a flea carrying a tapeworm that is concealed in the dog's fur.

What should you do?

Assume that your puppy is infested with tapeworms, and adopt a prevention campaign using a wormer recommended by your vet. Begin dosing your puppy as soon as he comes to live with you, and continue doing so at the appropriate intervals. I recommend my clients to worm their dogs against tapeworms every two to three months. Wormers are normally administered by mouth, but can be given by injection.

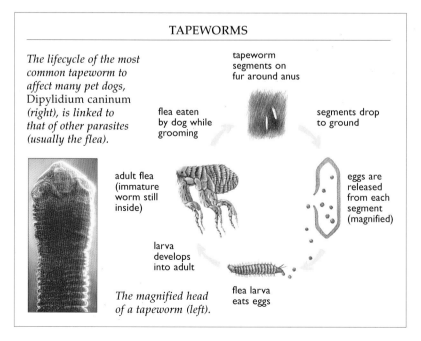

TAPEWORMS

The lifecycle of the most common tapeworm to affect many pet dogs, Dipylidium caninum (right), is linked to that of other parasites (usually the flea).

tapeworm segments on fur around anus

flea eaten by dog while grooming

segments drop to ground

adult flea (immature worm still inside)

eggs are released from each segment (magnified)

larva develops into adult

flea larva eats eggs

The magnified head of a tapeworm (left).

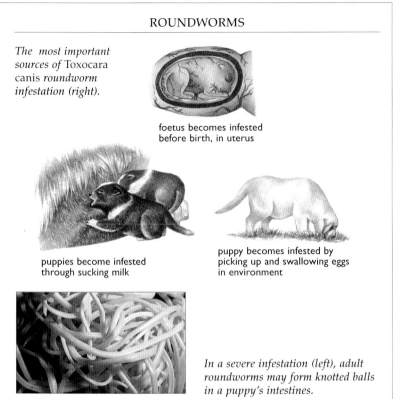

ROUNDWORMS

The most important sources of Toxocara canis *roundworm infestation (right).*

foetus becomes infested before birth, in uterus

puppies become infested through sucking milk

puppy becomes infested by picking up and swallowing eggs in environment

In a severe infestation (left), adult roundworms may form knotted balls in a puppy's intestines.

ROUNDWORMS

There are a number of types of roundworm, including ascarids, hookworms, whipworms, heartworms and lungworms. Perhaps the most common roundworm to affect dogs in the UK is an ascarid called *Toxocara canis*. Adult roundworms of this type have pointed white or cream-coloured bodies, and grow up to 15 cm (6 in) long. They live in an infested dog's small intestine.

How does a dog become infested?

There are a number of possible causes of roundworm infestation. Although some older dogs – particularly bitches after whelping – may have adult egg-laying roundworms in their intestines, most roundworms are found inside young puppies. Almost all puppies are infested by roundworms directly from their mothers, either before birth or immediately after it. Having been infested in this way, a puppy may have egg-laying adults inside his intestines by the age of three weeks.

An egg-laying adult roundworm may produce several hundred thousand eggs each day that pass out in a puppy's faeces. These eggs are extremely hardy, and may remain alive for up to three years. However, they are not capable of infesting another dog – or a person – straight away: in summer it may take two to three weeks, or in winter some months, for them to reach that stage.

The eggs may be picked up by the same or another dog, and will then hatch out in his intestines. Young, immature worms will find their way into the blood: some may pass through the liver and lungs before being coughed up and swallowed back into the intestines where they will become adults; others will go to tissues such as the muscles, where they lie dormant. In young puppies, the majority of worms take the scenic route through the liver and lungs, while in most older puppies and adults they take the alternative option.

Most adult dogs will have dormant roundworms in certain tissues. But a remarkable thing happens to the dormant worms in pregnant bitches. After about the 42nd day of a bitch's pregnancy, some of the immature roundworms become active once more, and find their way into the developing foetuses through their placentas. This is the reason why the vast majority of puppies are born already infested with *Toxocara canis* roundworms. The bitch will also pass immature worms to her puppies after they are born, via her milk.

What are the signs of infestation?

This depends on a puppy's age. An infested puppy of up to 12 days old may have noisy breathing and a nasal discharge, due to the movement of immature worms through his respiratory system.

In two-week-old puppies the worms may cause vomiting, diarrhoea and failure to grow properly.

Affected six- to 12-week-old puppies may suffer from vomiting and diarrhoea, and are often very pot-bellied (knotted balls of worms can sometimes block the intestines, causing serious problems). Dead and dying worms may also be visible in the faeces. These symptoms may occur in the worst cases, but most roundworm infestations in dogs go unnoticed.

Can people be infested?

Yes. People may unwittingly pick up eggs on their hands from the environment, and children may transfer eggs from their hands or other contaminated objects to their mouths. It is unlikely that a person would pick up eggs capable of infesting them by touching or stroking a dog, because the eggs take at least two weeks to reach that stage (see page 117).

Once inside a human's intestines the eggs will hatch, and immature roundworms will travel around the body. They may cause damage and disease as they move around, but serious effects are extremely rare. On average, there are only two recorded cases of *Toxocara*-induced disease per million of the human population every year in the UK. The following are all ways of reducing the chances of human infestation.

• Teach children good basic-hygiene habits: make sure that they always wash their hands before eating, and firmly discourage them from 'mouthing' objects that have been in contact with soil.

• Cover over any prepared food in order to prevent contamination by flies.

• Clear up all dog faeces immediately, before any roundworm eggs have the opportunity to develop to the stage at which they can infest dogs, humans or other animals.

What should you do?

Remember that your puppy will almost certainly have been born already infested with roundworms. Even if he has been wormed since birth, you should start using a recommended wormer from the time that you first collect him. The precise timing of worming will depend on the product and on the policy of your vet centre, but a common regime is to worm puppies at two weeks of age, and then every two weeks until they are 12 weeks old. After this age, most vets suggest worming every three months.

Wormers are available in liquid, tablet or powder form, and are given by mouth. Some products are effective against both roundworms and tapeworms.

OTHER TYPES OF WORM

Depending on where you live and your puppy's lifestyle, he may be vulnerable to infestation with additional types of worm. You should check this possibility, and the preventive action that you should take, by asking the advice of your vet or a veterinary nurse.

FLEAS

Dogs may become infested externally by a number of insects and other creatures, including lice, ticks and mites. However, by far the most common external parasite to infest dogs in many countries is the flea.

There are about 3000 types of flea, including the dog flea, but the most common type to be found on dogs is the cat flea. Under 3 mm (⅛ in) in length, fleas are remarkable little animals. An adult can jump up to 600 times an hour, and each jump is the equivalent of you clearing a 50-storey skyscraper in one leap.

How does a dog become infested?

Fleas live in the environment, not on dogs: to them, dogs and other warmblooded animals – such as cats and even people – are simply roving restaurants.

An adult flea will jump on to a dog to feed, clinging on to his fur and biting through his skin to suck blood using its needle-like mouthparts. A number of fleas are likely to have the same idea at the same time. While they are on the dog, they frantically mate and the females lay hundreds of eggs. After just a few days of living on the dog, the adult fleas die.

The eggs usually drop from the dog's coat to the ground within eight hours of being laid. A single flea larva hatches from each egg, and grows in size over the following weeks. When it is about 5 mm (¼ in) long, it spins itself a cocoon shell inside which it completely digests itself – brain, nervous system, guts and all – before building itself an adult body. As an adult, it can survive for about eight months while waiting for a dog or a cat meal to come along. The lifecycle may take up to two years from egg to egg.

The lifecycle of the flea

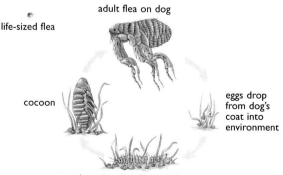

life-sized flea

adult flea on dog

cocoon

eggs drop from dog's coat into environment

larva hatches from each egg

In one form or another, a flea spends most of its life in the environment, only jumping on to a warmblooded animal – such as a dog or a cat – in order to feed and breed.

Your puppy may pick up fleas from any of the following sources.
• Directly from other dogs.
• Directly from cats (four out of five fleas found on dogs are cat fleas).
• Directly from other animals (such as hedgehogs and rabbits).
• From the environment in which any of the above animals live or visit.

The ability of fleas to reproduce is remarkable. If your puppy comes into your house with just 10 fleas on his back, within one month over 250,000 of them could have taken up residence.

What are the signs of infestation?

In your house • Fleas are visible to the naked eye so their presence may be obvious on your puppy or even on you (see below), but they are very fast-moving and it is unusual to spot them in the environment unless the infestation is very bad. However, just because you cannot find fleas in your house does not mean that they are not there: fleas are so common that it is likely that almost all homes that contain pets – as well as many that do not – have a resident population.

On your puppy • Some dogs are very sensitive to fleas, and are allergic to the saliva that they inject during their feeding activities. Even with only a low infestation of fleas in the environment, such dogs may show very marked signs of irritation, including scratching, and excessive licking and fur-nibbling. There may be tiny red, raised lumps on the dogs' skin where the fleas have bitten (these may feel as though sugar has been sprinkled in the fur), and they may suffer from dandruff.

On you • Remember that if a hungry flea is not able to find a dog or a cat, it may leap on to you for a snack. Having sucked some of your blood, it will jump off again and resume its wait for a dog or cat. You will be very well aware of the presence of fleas if you are sensitive to their bites. At the end of some evening surgeries at my vet centre in the summer, I have bites all around my ankles!

What should you do?

Ask your vet or a veterinary nurse for advice on the best flea-prevention products to use both in your house and on your puppy, and adopt a thorough flea-control campaign. Remember that fleas live mainly in the environment and not on dogs, so you should be sure to carry out the following measures.

• Regularly vacuum-clean and then wash all the items of your puppy's bedding.
• Regularly vacuum-clean your house. Putting an insecticidal collar in the vacuum-cleaner bag may help to kill any adult fleas that hatch out inside the bag.
• Regularly spray your house with an insecticide that is designed to kill adult fleas. Some products also stop flea eggs from developing into adults, and only need to be used three times a year.
• Regularly treat your puppy with flea products made specifically for dogs. These are available in a number of different forms, including sprays, drops, foams, powders and shampoos, as well as preparations to give by mouth. Flea collars are another good option, but must be changed on a regular basis to be effective.

TREATING YOUR PUPPY FOR FLEAS

As many dogs show a serious allergic reaction (known as a hypersensitivity reaction) to flea bites, it is logical to treat your puppy with a product such as a flea spray that kills fleas as soon as they come into contact with his skin, and before they have a chance to bite.

Other products – such as those designed to be given by mouth or as a few drops on the skin at the back of the neck – are absorbed into the bloodstream. These work well, but, because they rely on the fleas actually biting and then sucking blood in order to be effective, I would only recommend using them in cases where treatments on the coat are either inappropriate or are particularly difficult to apply.

Vaccination

All puppies are vulnerable to diseases caused by microscopic organisms such as certain viruses and bacteria, which may be rapidly and easily passed on from an infected dog to other healthy dogs. These are usually called the major infectious diseases of dogs; examples include viral diseases such as rabies and distemper, and bacterial diseases such as leptospirosis.

Vaccination improves the speed and effectiveness of a dog's immune system's response to a particular infection, by stimulating it through exposure to harmless amounts of the organism concerned before the dog encounters that organism for real.

Vaccination saves life

If a dog becomes infected by a particular organism, his body's immune system will react to try to destroy it, but the viruses and bacteria that cause most major infectious diseases are extremely quick to damage vital body organs and structures very seriously. Without vaccination, the dog's immune system may not be able to respond quickly enough to prevent him from becoming critically ill or dying.

In order to help protect your puppy from the major infectious diseases, you must ensure that he completes

Most vaccines are injected under a dog's skin (normally over the neck). The injection should only feel like a minor scratch, and few dogs seem to find it an uncomfortable experience.

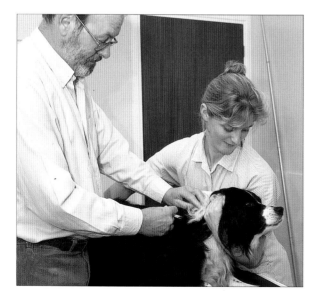

a vaccination course by the time he is 12 weeks old, and is then given regular 'boosters' every year (see opposite). Failure to keep up with his vaccinations will put him at risk. Remember that, in many cases, by the time a puppy is showing signs of the real disease, it may be too late for your vet to save his life.

WHICH VACCINATIONS ARE NEEDED?

The specific infectious diseases to which your puppy may be exposed will depend on where you live. For instance, the UK is believed to be free of the rabies virus, but in other countries the virus is widespread. The likelihood of your puppy encountering organisms that cause major infectious diseases will also depend on his lifestyle. If he visits places that many other dogs frequent, his chances of being infected will be higher.

Make sure that you discuss the specific vaccination requirements for your puppy with your vet. The major infectious diseases against which most vets in the UK recommend vaccinating dogs are summarized here.

Distemper

What causes it? • Distemper is a viral disease of dogs and other animals, including foxes. The disease is most common in areas heavily populated with dogs, and is transmitted through close contact.

Symptoms • These may include sore eyes, coughing, vomiting and diarrhoea.

Treatment • There is no specific treatment available, and the distemper virus is believed to claim the lives of many unvaccinated dogs every year.

Infectious canine hepatitis

What causes it? • This disease is caused by a virus that can survive away from a dog's body for up to 10 days. A dog may become infected through exposure to an environment contaminated with the virus, or through contact with an infected dog who will pass the virus in his saliva, urine and faeces.

Symptoms • These may include depression and anorexia, abdominal pain and bloody diarrhoea.

Treatment • There is no specific treatment.

Canine leptospirosis

What causes it? • This disease is caused by two related bacteria, whose lifecycle may cause severe liver and kidney damage. Bacteria in the urine of infected dogs are the main source of infection.

Symptoms • These may include depression, vomiting, jaundice and diarrhoea.

Treatment • An aggressive course of treatment that includes antibiotics may be successful if started early, but dogs may still pass bacteria in their urine for several weeks following recovery.

Canine parvovirus

What causes it? • A healthy dog may become infected by this virus through direct exposure to an infected dog, or through contact with his faeces. The virus can also survive in the environment for three to six months in certain circumstances.

Symptoms • Severe bloody diarrhoea and vomiting are the most common symptoms of infection.

Treatment • There is no specific treatment.

Contagious respiratory disease

What causes it? • Often referred to as kennel cough, this disease is not, in most cases, caused by a single organism but by a combined infection involving one type of bacteria (*Bordetella bronchiseptica*) and a number of different viruses, including canine parainfluenza virus. The severity of the disease depends on the organisms involved. The infection is spread by direct contact between dogs, and most commonly occurs in situations in which a number of dogs are sharing the same air space, such as in boarding kennels.

Symptoms • The most obvious symptom is a dry, hacking and persistent cough.

Treatment • Antibiotics and cough suppressants can be used to treat the disease, but recovery may take several weeks. The condition is not life-threatening.

WHEN TO VACCINATE

The precise timing of your puppy's vaccinations will depend on the specific products that are used by your vet, and on the current veterinary recommendations for your region or country.

For the first few weeks of your puppy's life, while his own immune system is developing, he should be protected from major infectious diseases by absorbing antibodies contained in his mother's first milk, or colostrum (she will have produced these antibodies either as a result of her own vaccinations, or through surviving natural infection).

The protection that is obtained from these so-called maternal antibodies will wane as your puppy grows older, and will normally have disappeared altogether by the time he is 12 weeks old.

NOTES ON VACCINATION

• Your puppy should be kept away from public places and unvaccinated dogs until seven to 10 days after his injection at 12 weeks (see below).

• The vaccinations from 15 months onwards are usually referred to as boosters. Your vet centre will probably send your puppy a reminder when he is due to be vaccinated. It may well be the only post he ever gets!

• Obvious reactions to vaccinations are unusual, but some puppies may be a little quieter than normal for 24 hours after being vaccinated. However, if you think that your puppy has reacted badly to a vaccination, contact your vet centre immediately.

• Vaccinations are not guaranteed to protect your puppy from the major infectious diseases, but it is rare for a puppy to fail to respond adequately to vaccination.

Your puppy's vaccination regime

You should expect your puppy's first vaccination course to consist of two vaccination sessions, several weeks apart. In the UK, a typical vaccination regime may be as follows.

At nine weeks • Vaccination against distemper, infectious canine hepatitis, canine leptospirosis, canine parovirus (and sometimes parainfluenza virus). All the vaccines will normally be mixed in one injection, administered painlessly under the skin by syringe and needle.

At 12 weeks • A repeat of the vaccinations given at nine weeks.

One month before kennelling • Vaccination against *Bordetella bronchiseptica*. This is administered by squirting drops of liquid into the dog's nose. Immunity from this disease may only last for six months, and repeat vaccinations may need to be given as and when necessary for kennelling.

At 15 months • Combined vaccination against canine leptospirosis, canine parvovirus (and sometimes parainfluenza virus), administered in a single injection. This vaccination should be repeated at 12-monthly intervals and supplemented at least every other year by vaccinations against distemper and infectious canine hepatitis.

Your vet should give you a record card containing details of all the vaccinations administered to your puppy. Keep this card in a safe place, and expect to be asked to produce it when you book your puppy into boarding kennels, or at any time by your vet.

Family planning

There is no telling precisely when your puppy will become sexually mature. The onset of puberty in a bitch is marked by her first heat, which may occur at any time between six months and two years of age. Most male puppies begin to show an interest in bitches in heat when they are about four months old.

Well before your puppy reaches puberty, you must consider whether or not you wish him or her to parent a litter of puppies in the future. If you decide that you would like to breed from your puppy, you should wait until he or she is physically fully mature. However, if like the majority of dog-owners you have no desire to hear the patter of tiny furry feet, you should decide on a permanent birth-control method to prevent a mating that could cause an unwanted pregnancy.

MALE DOGS

Having reached sexual maturity, male dogs can be sexually active at any time. Some cope well with their sexuality and their libido seems to remain low most of the time, but others find the restrictions imposed on their sexual activities very frustrating and may look for any opportunity to escape in search of females, or may regularly mount inappropriate objects.

Castration

This is a surgical operation to neuter a male animal. The base of the scrotum is opened and both testicles are removed, leaving a small wound that normally heals in about a week. Young dogs are generally castrated at any time after the age of six to seven

FEEDING AFTER CASTRATION OR SPAYING

Most dogs put on weight after being neutered because they require less fuel, or calories. Unfortunately, few owners are aware of this, and it is an important reason why so many spayed bitches and castrated dogs are obese. Monitor the weight of your puppy very carefully after neutering, and make any food reductions that are necessary to maintain his ideal weight (see page 63).

months: in most cases, the sooner the better. A dog may remain fertile for up to one month after castration.

Advantages
• Castrated dogs cannot father unwanted puppies.
• They are generally easier for inexperienced owners to keep under control.
• Castrating a male dog sets the example that birth control is not just the responsibility of bitches' owners.

Disadvantage
• Castration cannot be reversed.

BITCHES

For most of the year, mature bitches are not capable of becoming pregnant. But for a period of about three weeks, usually at intervals of around seven months, bitches come into what is referred to as a 'heat', or 'season'. During a heat, a bitch's reproductive system prepares for mating and possible pregnancy. The resulting hormonal disturbances often cause mature bitches to suffer from noticeable mood swings.

The reproductive anatomy of the dog and bitch

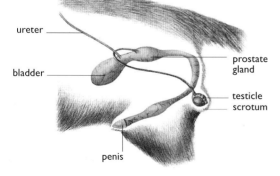

A healthy male dog has two testicles that will normally have descended into his scrotum by the age of six to eight weeks.

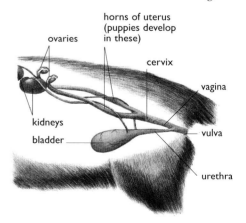

A bitch has two ovaries, one of which is near each of the kidneys. The uterus is Y-shaped.

The oestrous cycle of a bitch

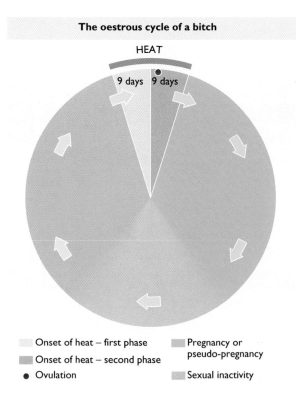

HEAT

9 days | 9 days

- Onset of heat – first phase
- Onset of heat – second phase
- Ovulation
- Pregnancy or pseudo-pregnancy
- Sexual inactivity

The oestrous cycle is the term given to the sequence of events that a bitch experiences from the onset of one heat to the next heat. If she is not mated, or is mated but does not conceive, she enters a phase lasting 70 to 140 days, for part of which she will be in pseudo-pregnancy (see below). She will then experience a period of sexual inactivity – normally lasting for about three months – before the onset of her next heat.

What happens during a heat?

The onset of a heat is marked by the production of blood-stained discharge from the bitch's vulva; this first phase lasts for about nine days. The bitch will be attractive to males, but will not let them mate with her until the second phase, which also lasts for about nine days. The bitch will usually ovulate (produce eggs) two days into this phase, but may mate for another week. Following a heat, a bitch will either become pregnant or will enter a state of pseudo-pregnancy.

Pseudo-pregnancy

In some bitches, this may go unnoticed; others will undergo physical and mental changes that are almost identical to those of real pregnancy, including milk production and nest-building.

Spaying

This a surgical procedure to neuter a female animal, in which the ovaries and entire uterus are removed through an opening created in the abdominal wall. Complications are very rare, and an uneventful recovery is normally complete within 10 days.

Advantages
- Spaying is a permanent form of birth control.
- It prevents the problems of pseudo-pregnancy.
- Carried out early, it reduces the risk of breast cancer.
- It prevents the possibility of a serious disease of the womb, common in older bitches.

Disadvantages
- Spaying cannot be reversed.
- Some bitches suffer from texture and colour changes in their coats (Irish setters and many spaniels seem prone to developing a 'woolly' appearance).
- Some dominant bitches can become more aggressive.

Birth control using drugs

Hormonal drugs can be used in the short term to suppress a heat, or to prevent a bitch from coming into heat on a longer-term basis. When the drugs are stopped, the bitch should eventually come back into heat. These drugs are only appropriate for bitches who have already had their first heat.

If you think that your bitch has been involved in an accidental mating, contact your vet. He or she will be able to inject hormones to prevent pregnancy, but this must be done 24 hours to four days after the mating.

If you would like to breed from your puppy, you should wait until he or she is two years old. Discuss your plans with the staff at your vet centre well in advance: there is much more to being a responsible breeder than many people realize.

A healthcare plan for your puppy

If you are anything like me, you will never remember when you should be having your eyes tested, your teeth checked over by your dentist or your tetanus vaccination updated, but now you have your puppy's health to look after as well.

Some healthcare tasks – such as feeding – obviously need to be carried out daily, and not even I would need reminding to do those. However, other important procedures – such as vaccination and worming – will be necessary at less frequent intervals, and can be easier to overlook.

The following is a checklist that will help you to create a healthcare year plan specifically for your puppy. Use the five-week example shown opposite as a basis for creating a plan that is customized to your puppy's first 12 months of living with you.

Feeding

What to feed • Feed your puppy a diet based almost exclusively on one or more high-quality, prepared 'complete' foods that have been formulated and properly tested to meet the nutritional needs of growing puppies (see pages 57–9).

When to feed • Feed your puppy three to four times a day at first, reducing to twice or once a day by the time he is one year old (see also page 64).

Changing to adult food • Gradually introduce one or more foods formulated and proven to meet the nutritional needs of adult dogs when your puppy is fully grown: the timing will vary depending on the size of your puppy (see page 67).

Water • Ensure that fresh water is freely available to your puppy 24 hours a day (see page 67).

Exercise

Every day, a puppy should be mentally stimulated as well as physically exerted (see pages 90–3). Tailor your puppy's exercise regime to his personal abilities and

---

TIMINGS OF TREATMENTS

Note that the exact timing of certain procedures and treatments will vary, depending on factors such as the nature of the products used and the prevailing views of the veterinary profession in your area or country.

Ask at your vet centre for precise information relating to your own puppy.

---

interests, and adapt it as he grows up. Remember that, while he is young, your puppy should not be over-exerted. Good exercise options include the following.
• Supervised indoor games.
• Controlled outdoor games.
• Walks on the lead.
• Controlled off-lead exercise.
• Swimming in safe water.

Grooming

At home • Give your puppy a quick groom daily, and a thorough groom weekly (see pages 110–12).

With a professional groomer • If you have a long-haired puppy, he will benefit from a professional groom every six to 12 months.

Bathing • Only bath your puppy when absolutely necessary (see pages 112–13).

Dental care

You should aim to brush your puppy's teeth and gums for one minute once a day, using an appropriate toothbrush and toothpaste (see pages 114–15).

Home health-checks

Inputs • Monitor your puppy's food and water intake daily for any obvious changes.

Outputs • Monitor your puppy's urine and faeces daily for any obvious changes.

Behaviour • Monitor your puppy's behaviour all the time: any sudden alterations may be early signs of illness. If you are concerned about a change in your puppy's behaviour, contact your vet centre for further advice.

Anatomy • Carry out a full physical examination of your puppy once a week (see pages 108–9).

Weighing • Weigh your puppy once a week. Do this at the same time of day on each occasion, and note down the results.

Veterinary health-checks

With a vet • Arrange for your puppy to be examined by your vet as soon as you have collected him at between seven and eight weeks old (see page 71), and subsequently at 12 weeks and 12 months old.

With a veterinary nurse • Your puppy should see a veterinary nurse regularly for development checks and weighing (ideally, these visits should be every four weeks until your puppy is 12 months old).

Vaccinations

Note that any vaccination regime will depend on the prevalence of diseases in your area or country, as well as on the products used (see opposite, below). The following is an example of a typical regime.

Against distemper, infectious canine hepatitis, canine leptospirosis and canine parvovirus (see pages 120–1) • An injection at nine weeks, a second injection at 12 weeks and a 'booster' at 15 months. (A vaccine against parainfluenza virus may be administered with the above.)

Contagious respiratory disease ('kennel cough') • Vaccination against *Bordetella bronchiseptica* at least one week before kennelling (see page 121).

Worming

Note that the precise regime for worming will depend on the predicted worm burden in your area or country, as well as on the products used (see opposite, below). The following is an example of a typical regime.

Against tapeworms (see page 116) • A dose at eight weeks; further doses every two to three months.

Against roundworms (see pages 117–18) • A dose at eight weeks, a second dose at 10 weeks, a third dose at 12 weeks; further doses every three months.

Faeces removal • Faeces should be cleared up quickly to prevent the development of roundworm eggs.

Treatment of external parasites

Note that this regime will depend on the predicted parasite burden in your area or country, as well as on the products used (see opposite, below). The following is an example of a routine treatment against fleas (see also pages 118–19).

On a puppy • An initial treatment at 12 weeks; further treatments every two weeks.

In a house • Treatment should be carried out before a puppy's arrival, and then every four months.

Family planning

Male option • Castration is usually carried out when a puppy is six months old (see page 122).

Female options • Spaying is carried out either before or after a bitch's first heat; hormonal treatment should start after her first heat (see page 123).

This extract from a typical healthcare plan covers the first five weeks after a puppy has been re-homed at the age of eight weeks. Use this example as a basis for developing a healthcare plan that is customized to your own puppy.

Week 8

clean teeth (daily) .... ☑
quick groom (daily) .... ☑
thorough groom .... ☑
health-check at home .... ☑
check weight ....date...............kg (lb) ....
health-check with vet.................................date............
development check with veterinary nurse....date............
first tapeworm dose ....date............
first roundworm dose ....date............

Week 9

clean teeth (daily) .... ☑
quick groom (daily) .... ☑
thorough groom .... ☑
health-check at home .... ☑
check weight ....date...............kg (lb) ....
first vaccination..date............

Week 10

clean teeth (daily) .... ☑
quick groom (daily) .... ☑
thorough groom .... ☑
health-check at home .... ☑
check weight ....date...............kg (lb) ....
second roundworm dose ....date............

Week 11

clean teeth (daily) .... ☑
quick groom (daily) .... ☑
thorough groom .... ☑
health-check at home .... ☑
check weight ....date...............kg (lb) ....

Week 12

clean teeth (daily) .... ☑
quick groom (daily) .... ☑
thorough groom .... ☑
health-check at home .... ☑
check weight ....date...............kg (lb) ....
health-check with vet.................................date............
development check with veterinary nurse....date............
second vaccination....................................date............
third roundworm dose ....date............
flea treatment .... ☑

Index

ACKNOWLEDGEMENTS

The publishing of any book is a team effort, and I would like to express my sincere thanks to the many organizations and to the individuals – both human and canine – who have played a part in creating *The Complete Guide to Puppy Care*.

I am particularly indebted to the following friends and colleagues for their advice, guidance and specific contributions.

Dr John Bradshaw BA Phd Director of the Anthrozoology Institute of the University of Southampton (the only research centre in the UK dedicated to studying the behaviour of dogs and cats).

Dr Anne McBride BSc. Phd Deputy Director of the Anthrozoology Institute and Course Director of the postgraduate diploma in Companion Animal-behaviour Counselling at the University of Southampton.

Erica Peachey BSc. (Hons) Consultant in animal behaviour.

Peter Young Award-winning professional dog-groomer.

Dr Jo Wills BVetMed. MRCVS Veterinary surgeon and animal nutritionist.

John Down BVetMed. MRCVS Veterinary surgeon.

Elspeth Down BVetMed. MRCVS Veterinary surgeon.

John Robinson BDS (Lond.) Dentist to the veterinary profession.

The publishing team Sam, Viv, Jane, Paul, Claire and Nina.

PUBLISHER'S ACKNOWLEDGEMENTS

Reed Illustrated Books would like to thank the following organizations and people for their help with photography, illustrations and modelling.

Mr A. Glue at Millbrooke Animal Centre (RSPCA), Chobham; Pet Plan Insurance; Craig and Janet Irvine-Smith, Sue Holden, Liz McGauley and Anne Walton at Stonehenge Veterinary Hospital; Waltham Centre for Pet Care and Nutrition; Wood Green Animal Shelter; Shirley Arthur; Geoff Borin; Jane Burton and her children; Vicky Gray; Jacky and her children; Rosie Hyde; Vera Lopez; Alison, Mike and Grace Molan; Claire Musters; Nicola O'Connell; Mr and Mrs Paul and family; Nina Pickup; Sarah Pollock; Steve Pound and Smudge; Michael Quinney; Tim Ridley; Helen Sargeant; Herb Schmitz; and Claire Tombs and Tyson.

Thanks also to Gwen Bailey for her advice on training, and for agreeing to the use of photographs from *The Perfect Puppy*.

PICTURE CREDITS

Animal Photography 43, 47.
Animals Unlimited 45 (centre below).
Jane Burton 12, 16, 17, 18, 19, 20, 21, 22, 23 (top and below), 24, 25 (below and top), 26, 27 (below and top), 28, 29 (top left, top right and below), 30 (top and below), 31 (top and below), 32 (top and below), 33 (top and below), 34, 123.
Bruce Coleman Ltd/Jeff Foott 55/Hans Reinhard 44 (centre above).
Sylvia Cordaiy/Paul Kaye 44 (top), 45 (centre above).
Dr Gary England/Royal Veterinary College 13, 14, 15.
Robert Harding Picture Library 98.
Image Bank/Jeff Hunter 113.
Oxford Scientific Films/London Scientific Films 116, 118/Carol Geake 114, 117.
Pedigree Pet Foods 58, 62.
Reed International Books Ltd/Jane Burton 53, 59, 64, 65 (top), 68, 69 (top and below), 70, 71, 72, 73, 75, 79/Rosie Hyde 38, 41, 76 (left and right), 77, 80, 81, 82 (left, top right and below right), 83 (left, below right and top right), 84 (left, top right and below right), 85 (left, centre and right), 86 (left and right), 93 (below), 94, 104 (top and below), 105, 106, 120/Ray Moller 44 (centre below)/John Moss 90/Tim Ridley 1 (half-title page), 3 (title page), 7 (introduction page), 10, 48, 54, 65 (below), 102, 103/Herb Schmitz 2, 9, 36, 39, 40, 56, 57, 60–1, 63, 66, 67, 87, 88, 89, 92, 93 (top), 95, 97, 99, 100, 101 (top and below), 108 (left, centre and right), 109 (left, centre and right), 110 (left and right), 111 (left and right), 112 (left and right), 115 (top and below), 119, 128. **Jacket photography**/Jane Burton (front)/Rosie Hyde (spine)/Tim Ridley (author's photographs, front jacket and back flap)/Herb Schmitz (back). **Illustrations**/Adam Abel 51/Stefan Chabluk 9, 15 (below), 35, 78, 103, 107, 123/Liz Gray 11, 12, 15 (top right), 16, 56, 116, 117, 118, 122 (below left and right)/Chris Orr (37).
Tony Stone Images/Jack Daniels 46/Chip Henderson 44 (below)/Jerome Tisne 49/Art Wolfe 78.
Zefa Picture Library 8, 45 (top and below), 91.

FURTHER READING

The Perfect Puppy by Gwen Bailey, published by Hamlyn (1995).